Henry VIII

Henry VIII

RICHARD REX

AMBERLEY PUBLISHING

First published 2009

Amberley Publishing Plc
Cirencester Road, Chalford,
Stroud, Gloucestershire, GL6 8PE

www.amberley-books.com

Copyright © Richard Rex 2009

The right of Richard Rex to be
identified as the Author of this work
has been asserted in accordance with
the Copyrights, Designs and Patents
Act 1988.

ISBN 978-1-84868-098-2

British Library Cataloguing in
Publication Data. A catalogue record
for this book is available from the
British Library.

Typeset in 10.5pt on 13pt Sabon.
Typesetting by FonthillDesign.
Printed in the UK.

CONTENTS

ABOUT THE AUTHOR

Richard Rex is Director of Studies in History at Queens' College, Cambridge and Reader in Reformation History at the University of Cambridge. He has written and researched extensively on Tudor England and his other books include *The Tudors*, *Elizabeth I: Fortune's Bastard?* (both published by Amberley Publishing), *Henry VIII & the English Reformation* and *The Lollards*. He lives in Cambridge with his wife and whichever of his six sons happen to be at home.

PREFACE

Of all the kings of England, Henry VIII has left the deepest impression on the imagination of posterity. The arrogant and colossal pose of the great Holbein portrait, which survives in so many contemporary and subsequent copies, conveys the awesome personality of a man who would still stand out even in the well-nourished society of early twenty-first-century England. Although this was just an image, created by the genius of Holbein, it was successful because it did not belie reality. Henry's sheer physical presence was remarked by his contemporaries, and goes a long way to explaining just how some of the political changes of his reign were possible. This was a man who could dominate the council table or even, on occasion, the Houses of Parliament: a man to whom it was difficult to say no.

After the portrait, it is perhaps those six wives of his who have helped him catch the popular imagination, which, as so often, has latched onto something of real importance. The six wives are not in fact the emblem of sexual prowess which popular fancy has made them – many kings have been far more extravagant in their amours than Henry, who had an acutely religious if almost athletically flexible conscience – but they do testify to his ability to move mountains in order to get his own way. Henry was a man who would overthrow a Church to obtain a divorce, a man willing to sacrifice ministers and friends, even wives and children, on the altar of dynastic interest.

This is not to say that Henry's reign is all image and reputation, or for that matter all blood and brutality. For good or ill, intentionally or not, his reign proved a turning point in English history. To his reign can be traced the roots of the Church of England, the seeds of the Irish Question, the birth of the English Bible, the founding of the Privy Council, and the principle of the omnicompetence of parliamentary statute. His reign saw the destruction of English monasticism, which had helped shape the society and landscape of England for nearly a millennium. As a result, it also witnessed the greatest shift in landholding since the Norman Conquest, and saw the landed wealth of the Crown itself reach its highest level ever. His reign, in short, saw something little less than a revolution.

1

EARLY LIFE:
1491 - 1510

Only one of the Tudor monarchs was born to the throne, and it was not Henry VIII. Born in 1491, his earliest years were spent as second in line for the succession, behind his brother Arthur. We know relatively little about those years, and myths have inevitably filled the gaps – most notably the idea that his father originally intended Henry for the church. No English prince had been ordained since the Norman Conquest, and the kings of Scotland had tended to use church offices to provide for their bastards, rather than for their legitimate sons. It would have been an almost shocking breach with custom if Henry VII had been contemplating an ecclesiastical career for his second son, and the idea is adequately contradicted by Prince Henry's installation as Duke of York at the venerable age of three (1 November 1494). His father would have been more likely to make him Archbishop of York had the church been the boy's destiny: royal and princely churchmen elsewhere in Europe at that time were often given exalted offices at a similarly early age, so that the church would bear the costs of their household and upbringing. Moreover, Prince Henry was brought up on a regime of martial exercises, becoming an expert horseman, which does not suggest that a priestly career was planned for him.

We do not know much about Henry's formal education, although the leading English poet of that generation, John Skelton, was employed as his tutor and later boasted of having taught him to write ('the honour of England I learned to spell') and presumably taught him his Latin. Skelton penned for his royal pupil a brief treatise on kingship. Like most examples of this genre, it was characterised more by sententious moralising than by practical advice, and it was framed simply as a series of quotations from suitable authorities. It was a long way from the subversive cynicism of one of the masterpieces of the genre, Machiavelli's *The Prince*, or from the almost equally subversive idealism of another such masterpiece, Thomas More's *Utopia* – both of them written before Henry was 25 years old. Skelton was soon to seem rather an old-fashioned figure, yet his teaching must have been sufficiently up-to-date, for his pupil's Latin prose style was later to be praised by none other than Erasmus, the greatest scholar of the age. Erasmus was introduced to the young prince on a visit to England in 1499, when Thomas More took him to Eltham Palace and promptly upstaged his nonplussed guest by presenting Henry with a little scholarly peace-offering – having failed to tip off Erasmus that it might be useful to take something along. Erasmus's subsequent goodwill offering was a poem in honour of Henry and his father, with a fulsome dedication to the young prince, encouraging him in his studies under Skelton's guidance.

Henry was evidently a talented and willing pupil, and grew up an accomplished man, speaking four or five languages, and able to sing, dance and play musical instruments. He wrote poems, and is one of the few English monarchs to have written a book – and in Latin at that. He dabbled in musical composition, writing songs and even, apparently, a setting of the Mass. Sadly, 'Greensleeves' was not by him, but 'Pastime with good company' certainly was. He was not above flattery on his musical talents. When Rowland Phillips, the Vicar of Croydon, and a frequent preacher at Court, earned himself a dressing-down from the king on account of a sermon which failed to please, the king's secretary wryly observed that he might have done better to imitate the example of the king's almoner, who that same day had preached to the royal household, by working in a few references to 'Pastime'. Music provided other ways to get at the king. A wandering Venetian friar named Dionisio Memo, a fine musician and a virtuoso on the keyboards, came to Henry's Court in the later 1510s, and was at once at the heart of its musical life. He was a particular favourite of the king's infant daughter, Mary. But the despatches of the Venetian ambassador during those years frequently provide information gleaned from Court by Memo, and it is tempting to speculate that the Venetian Republic had sent him to England precisely in the hope that his talents would purchase him ready access to the king and thus a fruitful supply of political intelligence.

Only with Arthur's death in 1502 did Henry become the heir apparent. And even then it was still possible, a year or two later, for the question of the succession to be discussed in terms which took little account of Henry's chances. For an unfortunate series of events that started with Arthur's premature death suddenly made the new Tudor dynasty seem newly vulnerable. Until 1502, the question of the succession seemed to be the one aspect of government over which the usurper, Henry VII, need have no worries. Himself a representative of the Lancastrian side in the 'Wars of the Roses', he had moved swiftly to marry the leading heiress on the Yorkist side, Elizabeth of York, a daughter of Edward IV. The 'Union of the Houses of Lancaster and York' was the keynote of early Tudor propaganda, which incessantly reminded subjects of the claim that this marriage had removed the very rationale for the dynastic conflicts that had plagued the later fifteenth century. That claim seemed to receive divine endorsement when their marriage was promptly blessed with their first-born, Arthur, whose given name is redolent with the high hopes his father had for him. Children continued to follow at regular intervals, including Henry (their third child and second son), so that, notwithstanding the high infant mortality of that time, by 1500 the succession seemed more than secure.

It was that sense of dynastic security that encouraged the 'Catholic Kings' of Spain (Ferdinand and Isabella, husband and wife, respectively monarchs of Aragon and Castile) to agree a marriage between their fourth and youngest daughter, Catalina of Aragon, and Prince Arthur. The four previous kings of England had all lost the throne by violence (though one of them, Edward IV, had managed both to regain it and then to die in his bed), and the last one to marry a foreign princess was Henry VI. The princely families of Europe were not keen to expose their daughters to such risks, and it was generally thought that Henry VII's execution of the unfortunate Earl of Warwick in 1499, after little more than a sham of a trial for treason, was carried out in order to reassure Ferdinand and Isabella, as killing him conveniently removed a potentially serious dynastic threat: Edward, Earl of Warwick, was the nephew of Edward IV, and thus the strongest Yorkist claimant to the throne. Perkin Warbeck, the Yorkist pretender whose bogus claim to be one of the 'Princes in the Tower' (the sons of Edward IV) had troubled Henry VII for most of the 1490s, was executed around the same time. With Warbeck and Warwick in the grave, the Tudors were safe from imminent dynastic threat.

Marriage to Catalina (whose name was anglicised to Katherine, today generally spelt Catherine) was in effect a coming-of-age ceremony for Arthur, and it was staged, like so many of the public ceremonies of Henry VII's reign, in St Paul's Cathedral – quite literally staged, as the royal couple walked above the crowds on elevated scaffolding so that as many as possible could witness the splendour of the occasion. The Duke of York had his part to play in the festivities, which were described in a pamphlet produced to commemorate the event. He welcomed her on her arrival at London and two days later, on Sunday 14 November, he escorted her from her lodgings to the cathedral for the wedding itself. Before Christmas, Arthur's training for adulthood was taken a step further as he was despatched to the Welsh Marches for an apprenticeship in government as Prince of Wales, residing in the royal castle at Ludlow, like Henry V a hundred years previously, the last teenage English prince whose father was still on the throne. But the apprenticeship was brief. Within a few months Prince Arthur had fallen gravely ill, and on 2 April 1502 he died.

Arthur's death was bad enough. But at first the gloom was lightened by the happy news that the queen was once again pregnant. Everything changed in February 1503 with the deaths, in quick succession, of Elizabeth's new-born daughter and then of Elizabeth herself. This was the context in which an informer reported to the king on a conversation in Calais about the prospects for the succession. A number of names were canvassed, and there was a sense that the Duke of Buckingham was the front runner. Young Henry's name, it seems, was not mentioned.

The loss within a year of both his eldest son and his wife was personally devastating to Henry VII, who never really recovered from the shock: he suffered severe and recurrent illness through the few years that remained to him. Politically, he became still more withdrawn and suspicious, and this showed in the difference between the treatment of Prince Arthur and Prince Henry. Henry's tutor, John Skelton, seems to have been pensioned off almost immediately (29 April) as the king drew his surviving son closer to himself. Arthur had been married at the earliest possible moment, and had then been sent off to train for kingship. But although the king hurried to betroth Arthur's young widow, Catherine of Aragon, to his second son – having secured the requisite papal dispensation to permit a marriage within what, by virtue of her first marriage, was now a prohibited degree of family relationship – he did not rush through the marriage itself. There was a theory at the time that sexual intercourse at too early an age could weaken the health, and he was not going to take any risks with his only male heir. Indeed, when in 1505 Henry reached the canonical age of consent for marriage (14 years), he registered a formal, though private, protest against the engagement which had been entered into on his behalf (though this was probably nothing more than a device of his father's to maximise his room for diplomatic manoeuvre).

Nor was there any question of Prince Henry's removal to Ludlow. Henry was kept at Court, under the watchful eye of his father. On the rare occasions when we see Prince Henry in the historical record, the king is near at hand. Henry might have picked up some hints about the arts of rule by watching his father, but he was given no opportunity to learn by doing. Thus when the king went on progress to Cambridge in 1507, the prince went too. The visit may well have made a deep impression on the young prince. The royal party was ceremonially welcomed in the very unfinished chapel of King's College, and the king was induced to promise funds for the completion and decoration of that great building. There was political capital to be made here, as King's College had been founded by the last Lancastrian king, Henry VI, who by this time was widely venerated in England as a saint, 'good King Henry', almost as a martyr, because of his sad fate – murdered on the orders of Edward IV. In his speech of welcome for Henry VII, the chancellor of the university related a story that must have been put about by the king himself, to the effect that when he had visited Henry VI's Court as a child, the old king had laid his hand upon the boy's head and prophesied that one day that head would bear the crown. By funding the completion of King's College Chapel, Henry VII was honouring his predecessor and emphasising his own status as Henry VI's legitimate successor. Young Prince Henry was to continue his father's work, by providing still more money to complete the magnificent stained-glass windows and carved woodwork of the chapel in the 1530s. Henry VIII had almost certainly been named after Henry VI according to the Catholic custom of naming children after saints.

Yet by the time Henry VII died in 1509, there were no longer any doubts. Even so, Henry VIII came to the throne at an uncertain age. Not yet eighteen, he was clearly an adult, yet had not reached that age of twenty-one at which, under English law, a man became formally capable of managing his lands and his affairs in his own right. This may go some way to explaining the almost occult politics with which his reign began. For while Henry VII died on 21 April, the news of his death and of his son's accession was not announced for another two days. In that interval, two of the late king's henchmen, Edmund Dudley and Richard Empson, were arrested, in what was a very public repudiation of the ruthless exploitation of feudal and judicial prerogatives through which Henry VII had filled his coffers. The two scapegoats were duly sacrificed on 17 August 1510.

For the first few weeks Henry's formidable grandmother, Lady Margaret Beaufort, the Tudor matriarch, looked like being the guiding force. But she soon followed her son to the grave, and could do no more than advise her grandson to pay heed to those mostly clerical royal councillors for whom she had the regard of a pious woman vowed to the widow's life: Archbishop William Warham of Canterbury, Bishop Richard Fox of Winchester, and her own spiritual director, Bishop John Fisher of Rochester. These men of course retained considerable influence in the first years of the reign, but it is not surprising that Henry's friends and advisers were mostly found among a group of younger noblemen, led by the Marquis of Dorset and the Earl of Surrey, and including Charles Brandon,

William Compton, and Edward Howard. They were his partners in the tournaments and pageants which enlivened life at the new Court.

The delicacy of the political situation and the inevitable cautiousness of churchmen were hardly a recipe for dramatic developments. The chronicle of the first years of the reign is therefore, not surprisingly, a tale of the arts of peace, taken up with the joys and festivities of court life. Common law may not have reckoned Henry old enough to manage his own affairs, but the law of the Church reckoned him old enough to marry, and his first move was to fulfil his long engagement to his brother's widow, Catherine of Aragon. The speed with which he did this shows better than anything that the 'protest' he had lodged in 1505 against his betrothal was nothing more than a tactical move dictated by his father. About two weeks later, fountains of wine ran for the people of London on 24 June to celebrate the coronation, as the king and queen were crowned together, like a couple in a romance of chivalry. Liberated from his father's smothering care, Henry threw himself by day into a career of hunting, enlivened at intervals by chivalric displays of jousting. By night, revels and dances were the rule. Edward Hall's chronicle of the reign tells us how Henry VIII and his companions dressed up as Robin Hood and his Merry Men for some Christmas frolics in 1509.

This happy phase of Henry's long reign came to a climax on New Year's Day 1511 with the birth of a baby to the royal couple. Better still, it was a boy, Prince Henry. King Henry was so delighted that he made a pilgrimage to Walsingham to give thanks. A splendid tournament was held to mark the baby's christening, and the king himself rode at the lists, shivering a number of lances. Tragically, the baby prince was dead within two months and was buried in Westminster Abbey. The Marquis of Dorset, who had led the knights at the tilts a week or two before, now led the mourners. Louis XII, King of France, had stood as one of the young prince's godparents, in absence of course (he was represented at the ceremony by his ambassador). But when he sent a letter of condolence via that same ambassador, one of Henry's councillors advised him against presenting it to the king, for fear of reawakening his grief.

Despite this heart-breaking disappointment, however, life at Court regained before too long the light-heartedness that chiefly characterised it in Henry's early years. There were Christmas revels every year until 1517, when the prolonged outbreak of a flu-like disease known then as 'the English Sweat' sent Henry into virtual hiding for half a year. Only in early 1518 did Court life resume. Nor was revelry restricted to Christmas. Tournaments might be held in any month from February to November, and pageants might be held at Shrovetide or in May. In May 1515, for example, Robin Hood was once more the theme. Catherine and her maids and ladies rode forth from Greenwich Palace one fine May morning into the nearby woods, where they found rustic bowers and tents and a band of masked men in Lincoln green, armed with bows and arrows. A vast outdoor entertainment then unfolded – with crowds of onlookers, at a suitable distance, numbering by one estimate some 25,000 people. The show concluded with a pageant procession back to the palace, featuring triumphal cars decorated with huge cardboard giants. In one respect, at least, the episode was a success. It must have been around this time that Catherine became pregnant with the only child of hers that would reach survive infancy. By autumn 1515 her pregnancy was common knowledge, and she gave birth to a daughter, Mary, in February 1516.

The sexes were most definitely not equal in Tudor England, and a daughter was something of a disappointment in comparison to a son. Nevertheless, Henry was happy enough with a successful pregnancy, and Catherine's place in his affections was safe – for now. As he remarked to the Venetian ambassador, Catherine and he were still young, and the birth of a healthy daughter offered reason enough to hope for a son. So Mary's christening was, like that of Prince Henry before her, an occasion of rejoicing. Sadly for the royal couple, however, the king's confidence was misplaced. Catherine was once more reported pregnant in 1518, but the child miscarried, and that turned out to be her final pregnancy.

2

WAR & PEACE: 1511 - 1520

In 1511 the king's mind began turning towards graver concerns of policy and war. The direction of his thoughts was fixed by his emerging conception of who and what he was. A convincing case has been made for regarding Henry as a practitioner of what has been called 'Renaissance self-fashioning': that is, the self-conscious construction of a public identity, or image as we would say. In the case of Henry VIII, that image was modelled on a royal predecessor, Henry V, as mediated for example through a biography translated from Latin and dedicated to Henry VIII in 1513. Henry V was one of the great exemplars of English, indeed of Christian, kingship, and Henry VIII had a lot in common with him. Each inherited the throne in the flush of youth from a middle-aged and unpopular usurper. Indeed, each inherited from a father who had outlived his usefulness through prolonged ill health. Thus each felt the need to establish his legitimacy and to secure his dynasty. Henry V pursued these ends through the zealous support of religious orthodoxy at home, and through a pro-papal ecclesiastical policy and a traditionally anti-French foreign policy abroad.

Henry VIII did much the same. At home, he presided over renewed repression of the Lollards, late medieval England's homegrown heretics, as Henry V had done before him. In Kent, Buckinghamshire, Coventry, and London (all traditional havens of Lollardy), dozens of suspect heretics were rounded up in what looks like a concerted policy. Most were induced to recant their erroneous beliefs, but a handful were steadfast to death, and were burned at the stake rather than agree to go against their consciences. The most characteristic tenet of the Lollards was their denial of the real presence of the body and blood of Jesus Christ in the consecrated bread and wine of the Mass, and this denial Henry regarded as a personal affront. As we shall see, he was always unhesitating in his commitment to the doctrine of the real presence.

Abroad, Henry looked to revive the glory days of the Hundred Years' War through an invasion of France. As a fit, strong youth, his head filled with dreams of glory and the great days of Agincourt, he was almost bound to enter upon war with France. Through the chronicles, and perhaps most of all through the 'Agincourt Song', Agincourt was still a living tradition, the ultimate testimony to the prestige of English arms. The myth of Agincourt was still potent when Shakespeare wrote his *Henry V* at the end of the Tudor century. When Henry VIII came to the throne, the battle was less than a hundred years past – as much part of the folk memory then as the Somme is now, if not more.

At first Henry faced an uphill struggle. His father had no taste for foreign adventures, having seen quite enough of

France during his years of exile, and the conservative and clerical council which he and his mother had bequeathed to the young king was not the sort of grouping to fling itself headlong into continental conquest. Now twenty-one, Henry was not to be gainsaid, and one of the ablest of the clerics broke ranks with his colleagues. Thomas Wolsey had arrived on the scene as a junior diplomat in Henry VII's latter years, on the coat-tails of Richard Fox, the Bishop of Winchester. He had a prodigious appetite for work, and seems in effect to have put his talents at the disposal of his new king, who in the company of his youthful jousting companions, men like Charles Brandon, William Compton and Edward Howard, looked forward to reviving the Plantagenet claims on French soil. Wolsey was the man who actually laid on the invasion, seeing to the tiresome details of supply and ordnance which were not the kind of thing gentleman-soldiers bothered themselves with. The emergence of Wolsey really marks Henry VIII's arrival at political maturity. The old guard of inherited councillors was edged out. Richard Fox (Lord Privy Seal) and William Warham (Lord Chancellor) soon betook themselves into graceful retirement from politics. Wolsey took the chancellorship, and his right-hand man, Thomas Ruthal (Bishop of Durham), took the privy seal.

If the driving force of the war with France was Henry's ambition for dynastic aggrandisement, the pretext on which the invasion was launched was the good of the Roman Catholic Church. Henry was able to combine self-interest with self-righteousness, making his invasion little less than a crusade. Louis XII of France, in pursuit of his own ambitions in northern Italy, had clashed with Pope Julius II, an enterprising reformer who believed that the renewal of the Catholic Church would be best served by a papal conquest of the Italian peninsula. In a quaint reversal of roles, while the Pope gathered armies to overcome the king, the king convened a council of the Church to depose the Pope. The Council of Pisa (1511) was something of wash-out – it was only attended by a handful of French bishops – but it gave Julius the chance to present his conflict with Louis as a religious war. He had already been cultivating Henry assiduously. In 1510 he had sent him the Golden Rose, an award made annually to a favoured prince. (Henry was so pleased at this honour that he rewarded the man who brought it with £100.) Julius's call for aid against France was a heaven-sent opportunity for Henry, and put his more peaceable clerical advisers in an impossible position. John Colet, Dean of St Paul's Cathedral and one of England's leading scholars, was a sufficiently representative figure of this party (though not at that time himself a member of Henry's council). When he took it into his head to preach to Henry's face on the subject of peace, the king took him aside and argued the case through with him, eventually persuading him that the proposed conflict was indeed a just war. True or not, the story illustrates the problem for anyone who wished to oppose the war. It must have been very difficult for loyal churchmen to argue the moral or the pragmatic case against a war which had been authorised by the Pope.

The problems faced in early modern monarchies by well-intentioned councillors such as Colet were deftly sketched out by his friend Thomas More in the first book of his masterpiece, *Utopia*, which is not only a description of a fictitious transatlantic commonwealth but also a satirical commentary on European, and especially English, politics. The book's protagonist, Raphael Hythloday, is invited by Thomas More to justify his refusal to join a royal council and thus place at the disposal of a prince his immense political wisdom, accumulated through years of study and travel. Hythloday explains that the sort of policies advocated by humanist philosophers such as him would be entirely unwanted in the councils of kings. While he would advocate peace and justice, a pastoral concern on the part of the prince for the common good or 'commonweal' of his people, the hearts of kings were set upon conquest and glory. The flatterers who surround kings would encourage them in their unrealistic ambitions, disregarding the fact that it was hard enough for a king to administer justice and promote virtue in one realm without adding another to his burdens. He illustrates his point with an imaginary account of a debate at a royal council table – tactfully making France rather than England his example. We should not mistake Hythloday's cautionary tale for an account of debates at Henry VIII's council table in 1512. Still less should we read them as an outright condemnation of the king and his policy. After all, Thomas More accepted a place on Henry's council soon afterwards, putting into practice the principle which, in *Utopia*, he maintained against Hythloday: namely that those in a position to do so should accept service with a prince so that, even if they could not attain the best outcome, they could at any rate work for the 'least bad'. But *Utopia* does offer us a fair reflection and assessment of the motives and interests which drove policies like Henry's. In turn, the war in France vindicates the critique put forward in *Utopia*.

War with France was a traditional policy with a good pedigree. The nobility and gentry flocked to serve with their king, doubtless sharing his confidence that it would all be as easy as it had been for Henry V. Archers and knights were the key to Henry V's success – along with the weakness of the French monarchy, where the king was a lunatic, and rival princely factions struggled for power. But the long French campaigns of reconquest against the forces of Henry VI offered a better lesson in warfare than the almost miraculous achievements of Henry V. The French reconquest was a matter of long sieges, with artillery the decisive weapon. English troops began to cross the Channel in the early summer of 1513, and Henry VIII joined them in Calais at the end of June. Moving out into the Low Countries in July, they soon found that conquest meant the long, hard slog of siege, not the short, sharp shock of battle. The 'Battle of the Spurs' (16 August) outside Thérouanne, in which Henry 'won his spurs' in a glorious rout of French cavalry, was no contemptible feat of arms. But it was little more than a skirmish, repelling a force sent to relieve a besieged city. Thérouanne was in due course taken and sacked, and nearby Tournai surrendered to avoid a similar fate. But at that rate the conquest of France was utterly impossible. It was only because the French king had ambitions of his own in Italy that the English made any impact at all. The sort of forces which Louis XII took into Lombardy in 1512, or which Francis I took over the Alps in 1515, would have made mincemeat of the English invaders. Nevertheless, Henry's war was successful, and nobody criticises success in war.

If conflict between England and France was traditional, so too was amity between France and Scotland. The 'auld alliance' rested on the principle that your enemy's enemy is your friend. Henry VIII's chief domestic concern once he had crossed the Channel was the prospect of a stab in the back from Scotland. To provide against this threat, he left Catherine of Aragon as regent in his absence, with Thomas Howard, Earl of Surrey, to provide whatever leadership in the field might prove necessary. Surrey, who had been one of the leading hawks on Henry's council, had been devastated to be left behind. He need not have worried, as he seized his chance for glory. No sooner had serious campaigning commenced in the Low Countries than the expected Scottish invasion materialised. James IV led over the border one of the largest Scottish armies ever gathered. Surrey marched to intercept him, and on the slopes and ridges between Flodden and Branxton, the Scottish king's tactical errors betrayed his forces to the greatest defeat the Scots ever met on English soil. James himself fell at Flodden Field (9 September), along with twelve earls and dozens of lairds and gentlemen. If we are to trust English estimates (which may well be inflated), then at 12,000 dead, Scottish losses were ten times those of England. Surrey's reward was restoration to his father's duchy of Norfolk the following year. The official English view of the Scottish king's fate was that it represented God's punishment upon him for taking arms against the cause of the Pope (and thus incurring excommunication). Henry had warned him in writing that he should not flout papal authority by allying with France, and his warning had been dramatically vindicated. John Fisher was called upon to preach a sermon to this effect, lamenting James IV's 'ill death and perjury'. It was not until absolution had been granted by the Pope that the King of Scots was granted Christian burial.

Despite his victories for the honour of his crown and for the defence of the Church, Henry found that he was unable to follow up his success owing to the collapse of the anti-French alliance in Europe which had made his invasion possible. His chief ally (and father-in-law), King Ferdinand of Aragon, was manoeuvring for peace with

France. The death of Queen Anne of France, though, gave Henry the chance for revenge, as he was able to offer his younger sister, Mary, to Louis XII as a far more attractive replacement. Ably assisted by Wolsey, who showed himself a consummate diplomat as well as a brilliant administrator, Henry certainly won the peace, though the value of his victory was reduced by the fact that the exertions of marriage to a demanding young bride brought the French king to the grave in a matter of weeks (a fate that provoked ribald comment across Europe).

The only lasting outcome of the war was the consolidation of Thomas Wolsey's position as Henry's chief minister. On the whole, things had gone well enough, and Wolsey's reward came in the form of a stream of ecclesiastical preferments. In 1514 he received in quick succession the bishoprics of Lincoln and Tournai, and then the archbishopric of York. The following year saw him add to this the Lord Chancellorship of England and a cardinal's hat (at Henry's request) from Pope Leo X. Wolsey was in the midst of the kaleidoscopic diplomacy of the next few years, alternately angling for war or peace at the lowest cost and maximum profit for his king. The stunning victory of the new king of France, Francis I, at Marignano in 1515, which gave him control of northern Italy, threw Henry's victories of 1513 into the shade and made peace the only realistic option. But at least the Treaty of London which Wolsey successfully negotiated in 1518, bringing together almost all the major international players, allowed Henry to pose as the peacemaker of Europe. Gestures like the recruitment of John Colet and Thomas More to his council enhanced this benevolent image, enabling him to present himself as an open-minded king prepared to give serious attention to the views of fashionable and at times critical intellectuals.

These years of peace excited the highest of hopes for the future. The Treaty of London inspired Erasmus to write to a friend in Basel, rejoicing over the fact that the four kings of western Europe – Francis I, Charles of Spain, Henry, and the Holy Roman Emperor Maximilian – had abandoned their ambitions to conquer each other's territories. It looked for a few glorious months as though the humanist publishing effort of the previous few years, which included More's *Utopia* and Erasmus's own *Institution of a Christian Prince* (dedicated to the young Charles), as well as Erasmus's epoch-making edition of the Greek New Testament, had really brought about the change of heart that the intellectuals of the age so earnestly desired. Of course, this same interlude of peace was the period which saw the emergence onto the stage of the man who was to do more than any other single individual to shatter the fragile cultural unity of medieval Catholic Europe: Martin Luther. But while his protest against what he saw as an immoral traffic in papal indulgences was heard across Europe, probably even at Henry's Court, no one could possibly foresee at that point that Luther, his theology, and the rival theologies that it spawned, would change the course of history.

Not that peace was Henry's real intention. He paid lip service to the treaty's proposal for a European crusade against the Ottoman Turks, who were steadily extending their hold over the Balkans and the eastern Mediterranean. Events soon demonstrated, however, that monarchical rivalries remained as intense as ever. The Emperor Maximilian died early in 1519, leaving the seven electoral princes of the Holy Roman Empire with the lucrative task of choosing his successor. The other three princes all threw their hats into the ring. As heir to the emperor's family domains (the Habsburg lands of Austria and Bohemia), Charles was favourite. But there were those in the Empire who resented the virtually hereditary hold of the Habsburgs on the elective title. This encouraged Francis. But he struck many imperial princes as far too powerful a monarch, a man who might have the potential to transform the Empire into a more coherent state, with a consequent weakening of the authority of the semi-autonomous princes. That in turn allowed Henry to seek to present himself as a compromise candidate. The election turned into a kind of auction, and Henry was the first to realise that the imperial title was out of his price range. He therefore lent his support to Charles, who eventually outbid Francis thanks to the support of the stupendously wealthy Jakob Fugger, the merchant banker of Augsburg. In 1519, the three kings may have fought out their rivalries in cash rather than blood, but the contest uncovered the emptiness of the dreams of peace.

Nevertheless, peace between Christian nations was the theme of one of history's most famous summit meetings, the Field of Cloth of Gold, near Calais, where Henry VIII met Francis I in person in June 1520. There had been talk of such a meeting for three years, but diplomacy and the imperial election had combined to keep delaying it. Beneath the genial gallantry and conspicuous consumption which filled three weeks of that summer so pleasurably, political tensions were mounting still higher. Henry's mortification at being cleverly thrown by Francis in a wrestling bout said more about their relationship than all the outward show. And the outward show was competitive enough.

(Henry's palace of painted canvas, one of history's most splendid temporary buildings, probably won the competition.) Even as he was going through the motions of international peace and harmony at the Field of Cloth of Gold, he was secretly negotiating with the new Holy Roman Emperor, Charles V, for a renewal of hostilities. War recommenced for England with a raid from Calais into Normandy during the autumn of 1522, followed by a more substantial but no more successful campaign in Picardy in 1523. By now, the expenses of war were pressing heavily on the English people, and objections to taxation were voiced in the Parliament of 1523.

Henry's ally, Charles V, shouldered the burden of the war in 1524, but his stunning victory at Pavia in February 1525, which reversed the results of Marignano ten years before, aroused Henry's martial spirit once more. Unfortunately for him, his people had reached the end of their fiscal tether. Wolsey knew full well that Parliament would grant no further revenue, so he endeavoured to finance yet another army with a forced loan, the so-called 'amicable grant'. The resulting tax-strikes and riots in Kent and East Anglia burst the bubble. The people were not as friendly as had been thought. Their objections to the levy were reported to the king and the cardinal by some of the weightiest political figures in the land: Archbishop Warham of Canterbury wrote from Kent; the Dukes of Norfolk and Suffolk wrote from those counties; and the Earl of Oxford wrote from Essex (his family seat was at Castle Heveningham). According to them, what Henry's subjects baulked at was the fact that the 'amicable grant' was being collected by men who usually collected taxes, on the basis of the assessments of wealth made for those taxes. In other words, they recognised at once that this was a tax in all but name, and they took their stand upon their prescriptive right not to pay taxes without parliamentary consent.

The sort of displays of dissent which marked the attempt to collect the grant would normally have been suppressed by a show of strength from the local officials and elites – sheriffs, justices of the peace, knights, and gentlemen. But of course on this occasion the elites themselves stood to lose the most. The 'amicable grant' was one of the most serious challenges to the traditional order of politics that Henry's regime ever mounted. Had the principle, in effect, of taxation without consent been established, the entire security of property of the landed elite would have been called into question. Without their cooperation, government was impossible. This impasse was what the archbishop and the other lords had the unenviable task of pointing out to Henry, and they themselves probably had as little interest as anyone else in seeing the primary power of Parliament, the right to grant taxes, subverted in this way. The king was facing little less than a rebellion, and a rebellion which some of his own closest advisers were, in the quietest possible way, encouraging. He had to back down. Fortunately, he was able to save face by blaming the whole affair on Cardinal Wolsey.

Henry's ambitions had outstripped his purse. But even as this phase of his reign drew to a close, Henry's attention was shifting towards the problem of the succession. His attempts to solve it, and the consequences of those attempts, would keep him out of military adventures for nearly twenty years.

3

DEFENDER OF THE FAITH: 1521 - 1526

Henry's piety and interest in religion had always been a matter for comment. Of course, medieval and early modern kings were expected to be decently religious. Nobody ever suggested that Henry's father was anything other than a loyal son of Holy Mother Church. Yet there were degrees of commitment even among kings. Henri III of France, who later in the century participated in public processions of penitential flagellants, was widely seen as taking his religion to extremes. Henry VIII was pious and conscientious without being extravagant. The Venetian ambassador, Sebastiano Giustiniani, sent back a detailed report on the young king, noting that it was his custom to hear three Masses on days when he went out hunting. If he was not hunting, he might hear as many as five. (The ambassador added that he was very fond of hunting!) These Masses would of course have been votive Masses, celebrated before side-altars or chapel altars by solo chaplains with minimal ceremony, not the full-scale High Mass of Sundays and religious festivals, with choir and organ, procession, and a platoon of clergy. Perhaps more striking is the ambassador's next remark, that the king usually said evening and night prayer with the queen in her chamber before retiring to bed. It might be tempting to write his piety off as so much hypocrisy, especially if it was just a matter of hearing many Masses. Even if it was perhaps hypocritical, it was far from cynical. Henry may have been at times obnoxiously self-righteous, spotting splinters in other people's eyes despite the heaps of timber blocking his own lights, but nobody could say he was not sincere. However, the little detail about nightly prayer with the queen tells us not only that his relationship with her was close but also that his piety was more than a pose.

More remarkably, but still acceptably in an age when, if it was understood that philosophers could hardly become kings, it was felt that kings might profitably endeavour to be philosophers, Henry had an educated interest in the faith he professed. In 1515 he personally intervened in the furore over the death in an episcopal gaol of Richard Hunne, alleged by the clergy to be a heretic but regarded by the citizens of London as a man victimised by the clergy for taking legal action against them in the king's courts. While the clergy maintained that Hunne had hanged himself, the coroner's jury returned a verdict of murder by his captors. Attempts to bring them to justice turned the episode into a full-scale dispute over 'benefit of clergy', the jurisdictional privileges of churchmen with respect to the law of the land. It was Henry who presided over a thorough airing of the issues involved and managed to cobble together a compromise solution. Henry loved theological arguments, and topics such as the value of mental prayer and the merits of Erasmus's radical edition of the New

Testament in Greek were debated in his presence at Court. When a preacher inveighed against Erasmus's work, Henry listened with barely concealed amusement while Thomas More engaged him in disputation and ran rings round him, and was delighted to learn that the only one of Erasmus's books that the preacher had read was, suitably enough, his *Praise of Folly*. Many books were dedicated to this intellectual among monarchs, and, if he did not always have time to read them himself, he would pass religious books to a couple of his chaplains for review and sit in judgement while they argued to and fro.

Henry's theological interests went beyond this dilettante dabbling. Famously, he composed a book against Martin Luther in 1521, when the radicalism of Luther's teachings had finally become apparent and had earned the German friar papal condemnation and excommunication. It was generally rumoured at the time, and has been generally accepted ever since, that the *Assertion of the Seven Sacraments* (as his book was called) was by no means his own unaided effort. There were at the worst of times troops of learned priests within hailing distance of the royal study, and it also looks as though he summoned professional theologians from Oxford and Cambridge to vet its orthodoxy and check its references. Besides which Thomas More was called in to apply some stylistic polish. Yet there is no disputing that Henry laboured upon it himself, for hours at a time in the first flush of enthusiasm. His secretary, Richard Pace, noted how much effort he was devoting to the task. We can see Henry's hand in the fact that the bulk of the book defends Catholic doctrines of the Mass against Luther. The Mass was a central and lifelong preoccupation of the king's. It may also be significant that, after the Mass, the sacrament to which Henry devoted the most attention was marriage.

Now, Henry had long been anxious to add a religious dimension to the English royal title in emulation of the 'Catholic' kings of Spain and the 'Most Christian' kings of France. The *Assertion* was dedicated by Henry to Pope Leo X, and after the text had been printed in July, a presentation copy was elaborately decorated and illuminated for him. Henry inscribed a dedicatory Latin couplet on the title page, and beneath the first page of the dedication there is a fine illumination showing a king kneeling before a pope and presenting him with a book. Beneath this, in turn, Henry signed his name with his characteristic 'Henry R'. The finished item looked more like a fine manuscript than a printed book, and it was sent to Rome with a batch of other presentation copies for cardinals and princes. The English ambassador to the Pope, John Clerk (Bishop of Bath and Wells), formally presented it to Leo before a plenary session of the cardinals, and then settled down to negotiating precisely what title would reward the royal theologian.

The accolade ultimately agreed upon was the *Fidei Defensor* (defender of the faith) which still adorns the coin of the realm. The Pope was no doubt especially pleased with Henry's comments on papal authority:

> I have no intention of insulting the pope by discussing his prerogative as though it were a matter of doubt... Luther can hardly deny that all the churches accept and revere the holy Roman see as mother and ruler of the faithful...

Pope Leo's untimely death that winter slowed down the process of issuing the 'papal bull' (the technical name for documents authorised by the papal seal or 'bulla') conferring the title. The bull finally reached England early in 1522, and the new title was formally bestowed upon Henry at a ceremony in Greenwich Palace on the feast of Candlemas (2 February) 1522.

Yet it should not be thought that Henry's aversion to Luther was anything other than heartfelt. In addition to the *Assertion*, Henry wrote a couple of other pieces against Luther. First of all there was an open letter to the Dukes of Saxony, urging them to suppress this troublesome friar before he did any more damage. A few years later he wrote a rather longer open letter to Luther himself – this, unlike the *Assertion*, was translated into English for the benefit of his own people.

The Catholic world was duly impressed by the English king's efforts, and the book went through several editions over the next few years. It was something of a bestseller, and was even translated into German (though not, at the time, into English, probably because Luther's ideas had not made sufficient headway in England at that moment to make it worthwhile). One of the translators, Dr Thomas Murner, a Franciscan friar, made his way to England in summer 1522 to present a copy of his translation to the king in person, earning himself the princely reward of £100. Another of Luther's prominent early opponents, Dr John Eck, who had engaged Luther face to face in a disputation at Leipzig in 1519, also came over to England to pay his respects to the royal theologian. His *Enchiridion* was the bestselling book against Luther of the century (perhaps of all time), appearing in over 100 editions. But the first edition, published in 1525, was dedicated to Henry VIII, who took pride of place in the list of sources from which Eck had derived his material. No doubt he brought a copy when he visited England in summer that year and was presented at Court, though his reward, at £20, was rather less princely than Murner's.

Catholic writers in general agonised over which to praise more highly, the king's learning or his virtue. That was the sort of reaction Henry had been expecting. What he was not expecting was the thundering riposte which Luther launched, his treatise *Against King Henry of England* (1522). The man who had braved papal anathema and imperial outlawry was not to be intimidated by a royal pen. Luther was quite possibly the only person who ever dared address Henry in such roundly offensive terms (even from such a safe distance). Henry found himself in the unwelcome situation of being impotent against defiance, and never forgave the affront. Luther's intemperate reaction had momentous consequences, as it ensured that, even after Henry himself had broken with the Roman Church, the Lutheran brand of Reformation would not find many friends in England. In the meantime, the task of dealing with Luther was delegated to Thomas More. Luther had lowered the discussion to the level of the dungheap, and More cheerfully kept it there, out-Luthering Luther in one of the most sustainedly and inventively vituperative tirades ever to be published under the guise of theology. The urbane author of *Utopia* was understandably anxious for this *tour de force* to appear under a *nom de plume*.

Henry had not merely gathered scholars from Oxford and Cambridge to vet and assist with his own book. He also expected his learned subjects to follow his lead in refuting the German heretic. While several of the university theologians are said to have written against Luther, only one of them actually published his effort. Edward Powell, a canon of Salisbury Cathedral, but also one of the theologians despatched by Oxford University to the king's aid, penned his *Propugnaculum summi sacerdotii evangelici* (or *Bulwark of the Gospel High Priesthood*) in 1523. But the most substantial work against Luther inspired by Henry's example was the *Assertionis Lutheranae Confutatio* (or *Refutation of Luther's Assertion*) of Bishop John Fisher, a comprehensive critique of almost every aspect of Luther's theology. Catherine of Aragon also backed her husband's campaign against Luther. Her personal confessor, a Spanish Observant Franciscan named Alfonso de Villasancta, published two Latin treatises against the new theology, one in defence of indulgences and the other in defence of free will. Both of them were dedicated to Catherine as 'Defendress of the Faith', an indication that she was as proud as her husband of his new title.

Nor had Henry himself retired from the controversial arena. In 1525, a strange and unaccountable rumour reached Luther to the effect that the King of England had had a change of heart and was now beginning to incline towards the cause of the Reformation. Endeavouring to seize the moment, Luther immediately published an open letter to Henry in which he apologised for the intemperate tone of his response to the *Assertion*. That book, he now suggested, must have been imposed upon the king by some subterfuge of Wolsey and the English bishops. Praising God for opening Henry's heart to the Gospel, Luther thus sought to mend fences with the man who would have been the most powerful ruler yet to adopt the Reformation. The rumour was of course unfounded, and Henry was stung to reply. Leaping adroitly onto the moral high ground, he graciously accepted Luther's apology for his earlier vituperation, before going on to urge him to recant his heresies as well as his bad manners. He denied with high indignation that he had developed any sympathy for Luther's theology himself or that the *Assertion* was anyone else's work but his own: he clearly had no intention at this point of sharing credit (much less blame) for his book. Although this letter, like the *Assertion*, was written and published in Latin, it is an interesting commentary on how things were changing that, in 1528, it was issued in an English translation.

4

THE KING'S 'GREAT MATTER': 1527 - 1529

Henry's theological credentials stood him in good stead when he found that he wanted a way out of his sonless and therefore burdensome first marriage, to Catherine of Aragon. Precisely when their relationship broke down irretrievably is unclear. In the years after 1510, Henry and Catherine were young and in love, but by the 1520s the age-gap was showing and the relationship weakening. The birth of Mary Tudor back in 1516 had given cause for hope that a son might yet follow, after the dreadful disappointment of 1511 and the intervening record of miscarriages. Catherine was again pregnant in summer 1518, and one of her maids of honour caught the king's eye. Elizabeth Blount played a prominent part in revels laid on to entertain some French ambassadors around Michaelmas 1518, and about nine months later bore Henry a son, whom the king acknowledged as his own. Meanwhile, Catherine's pregnancy proved both unfortunate and her last. By the 1520s her child-bearing years were clearly past, and her looks were fading. Henry was looking for pleasure in the arms of other women, and although the numbers of illegitimate children whom contemporary and later rumours fathered upon the king are hard to credit, there is no smoke without fire in these matters. His affair with Mary Boleyn, wife of William Carey, belongs to these years. After his experience with Bessie Blount, he may have decided that affairs with married women were more convenient. Quite how calculating he was is unclear. We do not know of many weddings that the king attended, but he did grace Mary Boleyn's wedding (4 February 1520) with his presence. Henry Carey, reputedly Henry's son, arrived in 1526.

Henry's decision to seek a formal way out of his first and failing marriage depended upon both a change of circumstances and a change of heart. The change of circumstances was the fortunate death in battle of the only potential rival for the English throne who was not within Henry's reach. Richard de la Pole, 'White Rose', the last surviving son of Edward IV's sister, having spent his adult life in the service of the king of France, met his death at the great battle of Pavia in February 1525, when control of northern Italy was wrested from Francis I's grip by the armies of Charles V. The Imperial victory was in itself good news for Henry, who hoped to make it the occasion for yet another invasion of France (Francis I had been taken prisoner in the battle, and France seemed ripe for the picking). But it was the death of White Rose which accounts for his instructions that bells be rung and thanksgiving processions be held throughout the land.

Only now, it seems, could alternative solutions to the succession question be entertained. This is evident in Henry's public recognition of his bastard son,

Henry Fitzroy, who was made Duke of Richmond and Somerset. These titles recalled both his Tudor and his Beaufort ancestry: Henry VII's claim to the throne had come through his mother, Lady Margaret Beaufort, who was Countess of Richmond and Somerset. The boy was also established in an independent household, at the castle of Sheriff Hutton in Yorkshire, with a little council to initiate him into the mysteries of government and politics. This was evidently following the pattern for the training of English princes, and for the same reason he was given a fashionably humanist tutor: Richard Croke who had taught Greek at Leipzig before returning to England to become the first native English professor of Greek at Cambridge, on a salary paid for by the king himself. So there may have been some thought of putting Fitzroy into line for the succession. If so, though, this would have been after Mary, not before her. For at around the same time she too was established in an independent household. Hers, like Prince Arthur's around 1500, was based at Ludlow, and she was in effect being recognised as Princess of Wales, a title which was sometimes used of her, though it was not formally granted. Mary too was given a fashionably humanist tutor, in the person of Richard Fetherston – a man who would stay loyal to her in the cruel years that lay ahead, and would eventually be executed for refusing to accept Henry VIII's Break with Rome.

It was not long, though, before a radically different solution presented itself: a divorce from Catherine of Aragon would free him for a second marriage. ('Divorce' meant not, as now, the termination of a valid marriage, but what is now called an 'annulment', a judgement that a marriage had not in fact been validly contracted.) By the close of the Middle Ages annulment was a familiar solution for the matrimonial problems of royal houses, and granting annulments was in effect a prerogative of the Pope in his capacity as Christ's vicar on earth. Many unhappy royal marriages had been terminated in this way – most recently and notoriously that of Louis XII of France to his first wife, Jeanne, after what amounted to a travesty of judicial proceedings sanctioned by the Pope. Pretexts for divorce could almost always be found. Complex family relationships within a relatively narrow élite obsessed with genealogy provided plenty of grist to the mill of Catholic canon law, with its intricate and extensive system of legislation and jurisprudence about marriage.

But Henry did not want a divorce on these terms. His case was far simpler, based on the text of the Bible and theological principle. It rested on biblical texts (Leviticus 18:16 and 20:21) forbidding marriage to a brother's wife, which seemed to cover his case exactly. He maintained that his marriage to Catherine was flatly prohibited by the law of God, that not even the Pope had any right to dispense anyone from their duty to obey that law, and therefore that his marriage, although originally sanctioned by a papal bull, was invalid.

Although initial discussions of the divorce were held behind closed doors, news soon leaked out. By May 1527, rumours were rife in London that the king's confessor (John Longland, Bishop of Lincoln) and other learned clerics had told Henry that his marriage was invalid. Henry ordered the Lord Mayor to quash the rumours. It was not long before wagging tongues were also talking of a daughter of Sir Thomas Boleyn, saying that if the king were once more free to marry, she would be his bride. Her name was Anne, sister of the king's former lover. This was the first that the public knew of Henry's change of heart, the other driving force of the whole process. As David Starkey has recently demonstrated, Henry's infatuation with Anne compelled him to seek a divorce, because she refused to tread her sister's path, and held out for marriage. It was to be a long wait. Henry himself always insisted that his doubts about his first marriage originated in scruples of conscience – but he was hardly going to say that he had gone off one wife and fancied another. He always preferred the moral high ground, and certainly convinced himself that he was acting from the purest of motives. His knack for combining conscience with convenience, self-righteousness with self-interest, made his wish for a divorce an irresistible political force.

Among the experts consulted about the divorce was, inevitably, John Fisher, whom Henry had once described as the most learned theologian he had ever known, and who was now renowned throughout Europe thanks to the powerfully argued books which, following Henry's lead, he had published against Luther. It was Fisher who threw the first spanner into the works, pointing out that the scriptural argument against the marriage was by no means clear. For the book of Deuteronomy contained a divine precept commanding a man to marry his deceased brother's wife when that brother had died without children (Deut. 25:5). This special case exactly described the case of Henry, his brother Arthur, and Catherine of Aragon. From that point on, the debate over Henry's marriage, which sucked in scholars from all over Europe for nearly ten years, concentrated on the problem of relating the prohibition in Leviticus to the injunction in Deuteronomy. Ultimately, it would be politics rather than theology which decided the issue.

But Henry not only liked to win, he liked to be in the right. So enormous efforts went into trying to put him there.

The text of Deuteronomy which Fisher put into play made it far harder for Henry to keep the theological high ground, and might have become an embarrassment had not an ambitious young Cambridge don come up with some answers. Robert Wakefield – ironically a former protégé of Fisher's – was Tudor England's leading expert in Hebrew. On first being asked for an opinion in 1527, he wisely replied that he would not offer one until he had Henry's clear instructions to do so. His request for formal authorisation was shrewd enough: under the Tudors, academic discussions about the royal succession could easily be construed as treason. More to the point, he wanted to know what answer the king wanted. Wakefield's skill in Hebrew enabled him to deliver the goods. The prohibition in Leviticus had a curse attached to it, warning anyone who married his brother's wife that he would be 'without children'. As Henry had a child, Mary, this had not seemed very helpful until Wakefield observed, rightly, that in context this had to mean without sons to carry on the family name. Moreover, he argued, while Leviticus was speaking of full brothers, Deuteronomy was using the word 'brother' in the wider sense of male relatives in general. He therefore proposed that Leviticus was prohibiting one special case of the general obligation imposed in Deuteronomy. This was not watertight, but it would do. And now Henry saw himself as the victim of a providential punishment in the miscarriages or deaths of his lost sons, he was more than ever convinced that his understanding of Leviticus was correct, no matter what Deuteronomy might say.

1. Greenwich Palace. Massively and expensively rebuilt by Henry VII, Greenwich Palace was the birthplace of Henry VIII and a favoured residence of all the Tudors.

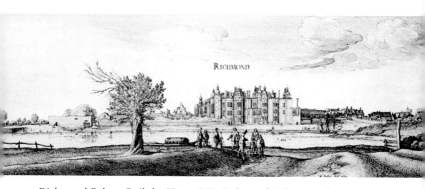

RICHMOND

2. Richmond Palace. Built by Henry VII, Richmond Palace was home to Henry VIII for much of his childhood.

Next pages: 3. & 4. Henry VII and Elizabeth of York. Henry VIII's parents, in later copies of the matched pair of portraits in the Royal Collection. As in the originals, they are shown holding respectively the Red Rose of Lancaster and the White Rose of York, to symbolise the union of the houses after the 'Wars of the Roses'.

HENRICVS. VII.

ꟼIZABETHA VXOR HENRICI.S VII.

 EDWARDVS. IIII.

RICARDVS. III.

7. Henry VII's chantry chapel in Westminster Abbey. This elaborate bronze structure houses the tombs of Henry and Elizabeth. Until the reign of Edward VI, it also contained a fine altar dedicated to Jesus, at which the daily Masses for their souls were to be said.

Previous page: 5. Edward IV. Although Henry's resemblance to his maternal grandfather, Edward IV, was remarked upon, it is not evident from this poor later copy.

Previous page: 6. Richard III. Richard III, defeated and killed at Bosworth Field in 1485, was subsequently demonised by Tudor propagandists. His alleged hunchback is clearly depicted in this heavily lopsided later copy of an authentic portrait.

Opposite: 8. Lady Margaret Beaufort. The matriarch of the Tudor dynasty, through whom Henry VII derived his tenuous claim to the throne, Lady Margaret narrowly outlived her son, to die early in her grandson's reign. Like her son, she is buried in what is in effect the Tudor mausoleum, the Lady Chapel he built at the back of Westminster Abbey.

MARGARETA · MATER · HENRICI · VII

Above: 9. Great Tournament Roll of Westminster. Henry VIII riding at the tilts with Catherine of Aragon looking on, at the tournament held in the Westminster tiltyard, 12-13 February 1511, to mark the birth of the shortlived Prince Henry. Henry's horse wears a blue 'bard' ornamented with K for Katherine (the contemporary spelling) and with the word Loyall in gold letters on the border.

Below: 10. A view of Westminster, ca. 1550, by Anthony van den Wyngaerde. Although the King's Court remained highly peripatetic under Henry VIII, Westminster was already the nearest thing to a fixed capital for English government.

11. Parliament Roll, 1512 (later copy). The young king is shown in the procession for the opening of the 1512 Parliament, walking beneath a ceremonial canopy of blue and gold blazoned with a Tudor rose.

12. Coronation of Henry VIII. In this image, copied from an illuminated initial in the mortuary roll (1532) of John Islip, Abbot of Westminster (1500-1532), we see the abbey itself, cut open to give a view of what was perhaps the highlight of Abbot John's life: the coronation of Henry VIII in the abbey church on 24 June 1509.

13. Henry VIII meets the Emperor Maximilian I. This painting, made for the king to commemorate his campaign in France in 1513, shows the meeting between Henry (on the right) and the Holy Roman Emperor Maximilian I (on the left). Henry's tent is marked with the royal arms, Maximilian's with the Habsburg double-headed eagle.

14, 15. & 16. Henry VIII's Great Seals. The Great Seal, which was usually in the custody of the Lord Chancellor, was the ultimate instrument of authentication for acts of royal power in Tudor England, and was affixed, for example, to treaties and charters. It depicted the king enthroned in majesty on the front, and riding into battle on the back, symbolising his power as fount of justice and leader in war. In the first two versions of the seal (from the start of the reign and from the 1520s), the image of the seated king makes no pretensions of giving a likeness and the design is Gothic in style, but in the final version, struck in the 1540s, a recognisable Henry VIII is enthroned in a Renaissance background (bottom right).

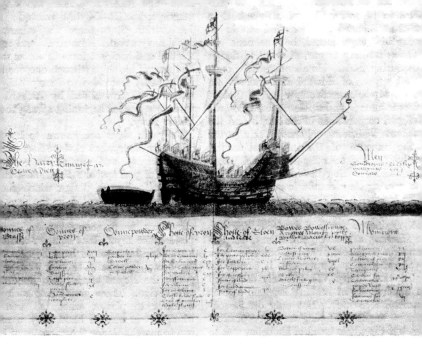

17. The *Harry Grâce à Dieu*. After one of his favourite ships had been sunk in battle in 1512, Henry 'caused a greate shippe to be made, suche another as was neuer seen before in Englande, and called it, Henry grace de dieu'. One of Henry's greatest vessels, it was launched amid great ceremony on 25 October 1515. Henry, Catherine (by then obviously pregnant), and the Court enjoyed a splendid banquet aboard.

Above left: 18. Cardinal Wolsey. This drawing, which survives at Arras, probably dates from the mid-1510s, when Wolsey was trying to vindicate his claim to be bishop of Tournai, which Henry had captured in the campaign of 1513. Wolsey is not yet the obese figure of the more familiar likenesses.

Above right: 19. Illuminated initial from the Plea Rolls, 1514. Royal documents were often decorated with illuminated initials depicting the king on his throne. Here he is shown with a small group of councilors.

21. The Field of Cloth of Gold. This contemporary painting recorded some of the highlights of Henry's meeting with Francis I, which was a curious combination of a summit conference with an international sporting event and a fashion show. Henry's palace, one of history's most splendid temporary buildings, stands centre right, and the dragon (top left) alludes to one of the more spectacular fireworks that were set off.

22. *Pastyme with good companye*. Henry VIII's most famous song (for he did not write *Greensleeves*!) as found in the 'Henry VIII Songbook'. *Pastyme* has a catchy enough tune, but slightly sententious lyrics.

Opposite: 20. Erasmus. This iconic woodcut by Dürer depicts the greatest scholar of the age, Desiderius Erasmus of Rotterdam, at work in his study. The Latin inscription states that the image was sketched from life by Dürer, while the Greek beneath it assures the select few who can read it that Erasmus's writings give an even truer picture of the great man.

Above and below: 23. & 24. The Field of Cloth of Gold. Two bas reliefs from the 1520s, depicting scenes from the meeting between Henry VIII and Francis I. They are part of a set of five panels that decorate the Galerie d'Aumale in the Hôtel de Bourgtheroulde, a noble townhouse in Rouen.

Above, Henry VIII's party sets out from Guines; below, the royal parties meet, with Henry approaching from the left and Francis from the right. Note the English horseman at the far left, armed with a longbow.

25. An English Lady, by Holbein. This front and back view of a lady in English costume probably dates from Holbein's first visit to England in the 1520s. Note the prominent set of rosary beads that hangs from her girdle.

Middle and below: 26. & 27. John More and Anne Cresacre, by Holbein. These sketches were both preliminary drawings for the group portrait of More's family. Anne Cresacre joined More's family as his ward after her father's death, and in 1529 she was married to More's son, John.

29. Elizabeth Dauncey,
by Holbein. The
erroneous label 'The
Lady Barkley' was
added later. This is
another preliminary
study for the group
portrait of More's
family, and shows
his second daughter
Elizabeth, who married
a courtier named
William Dauncey.

30. Golden Bull of Pope Clement VII. The papal 'bull', or seal, was usually formed in lead, but on special occasions, as here, they were formed in gold. This one, designed by the great Benvenuto Cellini, was affixed to Clement VII's bull confirming Henry VIII's title as *Fidei Defensor*. Like all papal bulls, it shows the twin founders of the Church of Rome, the apostles Peter and Paul.

Opposite: 33. In this typical 'long gallery' copy, of the kind that was mass produced in late Tudor and Stuart England to decorate the homes of the aristocracy, Catherine of Aragon is shown in middle age, at about the time that Henry's eye began to wander more widely.

31. Holbein's design for a jeweled pendant for Princess Mary, probably done during his first visit to England (1526-28), when Mary was still in favour and was perhaps even being groomed for possible succession to the throne.

32. Anne Boleyn's clock. One of many artifacts that testify to Henry's affection for Anne, this clock, given to Anne by the king, has the initials 'H. A.' marked on its weights.

36. Treaty of Amiens, 18 August 1527. Cardinal Wolsey personally negotiated this wide-ranging treaty with France on a lengthy embassy there in the summer of 1527. The ostensible aims of the treaty were to free the Pope from virtual captivity by imperial forces, and failing that, to transfer the government of the Catholic Church temporarily to a committee of cardinals led by Wolsey himself. Behind this, of course, was the pressing need to secure Henry VIII's divorce one way or another. But Wolsey's prolonged absence enabled other political voices to gain access to the king's ear.

Previous page: 34. Henry VIII at his physical peak in the early 1520s, around the time of his affair with Mary Boleyn, when the gap in age between him and his queen was beginning to show.

Previous page: 35. Mary Boleyn, Anne's elder sister, was Henry VIII's mistress in the early 1520s. Her first husband, William Carey, whom she had married in 1520, received a handsome series of grants of land and office between 1522 and 1525, and Henry named a ship after Mary in 1523. The Careys' son Henry, born in 1526, was widely rumoured to have been fathered by the king.

37. Hampton Court. On Wolsey's fall, his vast wealth and property fell into Henry's hands. Among the prizes was Hampton Court, here shown as subsequently completed by the king.

38. Letter from Anne Boleyn to Wolsey. In this letter Anne thanks Wolsey for his great services in her cause, and promises that if, after the attainment of her hopes, there is anything in the world she can do for him, 'you shall fynd me the gladdyst woman in the woreld to do yt'.

39. A letter from Wolsey to the king, October 1529. Undated, but written in the wake of his sudden fall from favour on 9 October, this letter begs Henry for 'grace mercy remyssyon and pardon' in abject terms as his 'moste prostrat poor chapleyn creature and bedesman'.

While the theological aspects of the divorce were being investigated, there were other paths to be pursued. The divorce would require political support, and this would have to come from France. So Cardinal Wolsey himself set off on a rare personal mission abroad, to consolidate new contacts with the French king, who was to be a reliable and helpful ally for the next ten years. Although Wolsey inevitably used the journey as a symbolic statement of his own grandeur, travelling in state with a vast household, he ought to have realised that an embassy, however exalted, meant absence from the king's presence, which, in a personal monarchy, in turn meant political risk. After all, he had himself used diplomatic missions as a way of removing potential rivals from Court, most notably in sending the royal secretary, Richard Pace, to Switzerland and then Italy in the early 1520s, a move which severed the special relationship that Pace had been developing with the king. In Wolsey's absence, Henry was receptive to advice from other quarters, and after his return the cardinal never quite regained his former control of the agenda of government (although had he managed to secure Henry his divorce, his ascendancy would once more have become total).

Dissolving marriages was the Pope's business, and Henry naturally expected the Pope to co-operate. From his point of view, that was what the Pope was for. Henry had generally supported papal diplomacy during his reign, most notably in the early conflict with France, and even in the 1510s had reckoned that his influence counted for a great deal in Rome. Since then he had lent his considerable prestige to buttress papal authority by writing in person against Luther. Now it was time to call in the debt. Characteristically, Henry was oblivious to the obstacles in his path. First, the Imperial victory at Pavia which had given Henry the incentive to seek a divorce denied him the means to get one. For it left Charles V in control of Italy. Imperial armies went on to sack Rome in 1527, making the Pope a virtual prisoner in his own fortress of Castel Sant'Angelo. Clement VII was in no position to offend the Emperor by granting Henry a divorce which would proclaim that Charles V's aunt had been living in incest for nearly twenty years. (Sixteenth-century Europe was a man's world, in which sexual disgrace attached itself far more readily to women than to men.) The second obstacle was Catherine's own acute sense of honour and dignity. While these royal matrimonial problems could be sorted out amicably if the woman was prepared to accept a kind of respectable retirement, Catherine would not give an inch, and she was every inch a Spanish princess. Finally, as his first marriage had itself required a papal dispensation from canon law (which, like Leviticus, forbade marriage to a sister-in-law), Henry was asking the Pope to reverse a decision by a recent predecessor. While this was not beyond the bounds of possibility, it would have been very bad timing in the 1520s. The Protestant Reformation then gaining ground in Germany and Switzerland was not only challenging papal authority in principle (denying that Christ had granted St Peter or his successors any special authority in the Church) but also impugning it in practice, arguing that its judicial proceedings were corrupted by wealth and power. Not exactly the moment to overturn an earlier papal bull in order to do a favour to a friendly king.

The Pope's only option was to play for time in the hope that death would solve his problem. Almost anybody's death would have done: Charles, Henry, Catherine, or Anne Boleyn. In the meantime, he strung Henry along, for if he could not risk offending Charles V by granting the divorce, no more could he afford to alienate Henry by ruling it out. So when royal envoys suggested having the case tried at a special court in London, he played along, and sent Cardinal Campeggio to preside with Cardinal Wolsey. Campeggio knew the rules of the game, and it was six months after his arrival before the court finally convened in June 1529.

Although the legal proceedings were short and inconclusive, they were packed with incident. Catherine attempted to pull the plug right at the start. She maintained, reasonably enough, that she could hardly expect a fair hearing in her estranged husband's capital city, and therefore appealed to the Pope to have the case revoked to Rome. As Henry was also present, Catherine's behaviour was a mortal insult, a blow to that image of fair-mindedness which he had cultivated so assiduously. Despite her pre-emptive strike, there followed a desultory airing of the arguments over the marriage itself by representatives of the king and queen. The formal statement of Henry's case was presented to the legates in writing (lost and forgotten for centuries, it was rediscovered in the 1980s by Dr Virginia Murphy in the library of Trinity College, Cambridge), as were various supporting treatises by scholars such as Robert Wakefield and Stephen Gardiner.

One of the documents produced in court led to another uncomfortable scene. It was a letter addressed to the Pope and signed by a number of English bishops, petitioning for a prompt resolution to the king's suit, affirming that his concerns arose from genuine conscientious scruples, and generally implying support for his position. The first signatory was the Archbishop of Canterbury, and the second was, surprisingly, the Bishop of Rochester, John Fisher, the leading scholar at work on Catherine's side. However, no sooner was his name read out than he protested loudly that he had never signed such a letter, and that his signature and his seal were frauds or forgeries. This was another slight upon the king's honour, as it was not at all good for the king to be associated with such sharp practice. And sharp practice it was. Fisher's signature was customarily 'Jo Roffs', short for 'Johannes Roffensis' ('John of Rochester'). But the signature on the document is given in the form 'Jo Roffensis': it is not his. It is unlikely that Henry had any responsibility for this inept subterfuge. But it was not good for his reputation.

Worse was to come. Making an impassioned speech in defence of the validity of the royal marriage, Fisher was so far carried away as to proclaim that he would be prepared to give his life, like John the Baptist, in defence of the marriage bond. This was triply offensive to the king, who was present when Fisher spoke. Firstly, it begged the question: the whole point of the tribunal was to ascertain whether the marriage bond was valid or not. Secondly, it cut both ways. John the Baptist had been murdered on the orders of King Herod for protesting when Herod divorced his wife in order to marry Herodias, formerly his brother's wife. Henry's scholars liked to quote this story as evidence that you could not marry your brother's wife! But worst of all was the subtext: if John Fisher was John the Baptist, then Henry was Herod.

Campeggio suspended the court and referred the case back to Rome. Catherine's appeal was his pretext, but his decision was more to do with Italian politics than anything else. For a year or more the French had been trying to prise Italy from Imperial hands. The last throw of the dice came in June 1529 at Landriano in the Po Valley. A French army marching south to relieve other French forces under siege near Naples was cut to pieces by Imperial troops, and papal diplomacy was left in tatters.

5

TURNING AGAINST THE CLERGY: 1530 - 1532

The revocation of the case to Rome infuriated Henry, who responded, as so often when baulked of his heart's desire, by lashing out. In this case the target was Cardinal Wolsey. His career had been built on giving the king what he wanted, and his precipitous fall was the price of failure. Fifteen years at the top had left Wolsey with enemies galore, and the predators who led the attack at court and then in the Parliament which Henry summoned that autumn were followed by the carrion birds who flocked in for the pickings. The lands and offices which Henry was able to redistribute that autumn doubtless helped convince many English gentlemen of the righteousness of his cause. Not that he took Wolsey's head straightaway. The cardinal was rusticated to the diocese of York, which he had held since 1514 but never visited. It was only his mistaken belief that he could remain a player in European politics despite having lost the king's favour that finally destroyed him. His private contacts with representatives of Charles V were almost calculated to offend Henry, who certainly did not think foreign affairs a proper arena for the meddling of unauthorised subjects. Summoned to London in 1530 to face charges of treason, Wolsey cheated the headsman by dying on his journey south.

The fall of Wolsey in 1529 was accompanied by a clutch of statutes nibbling away at the privileges and interests of the clergy. Catherine of Aragon enjoyed a good deal of support among the clergy, and the constant pressure put upon them over the next few years was designed not only to intimidate the Pope but also to bring the clergy at home into line. When three English bishops (and supporters of hers) appealed to Rome against these statutes, they were promptly imprisoned. To crown it all, the whole body of the English clergy was fined an astronomical £100,000 for having breached the ancient statute of 'praemunire' through being accomplices, so to speak, in Wolsey's exercise of his powers as papal legate in England over the previous ten or fifteen years. The Defender of the Faith was beginning to attack the Church. A year or so later, a discontented friar described him as the 'Destroyer of the Faith'.

Meanwhile, Henry's scholars were on overtime. Some were detailed to work on Thomas More, whom Henry had appointed Lord Chancellor in succession to Wolsey. In the complex matter of the divorce there was no one whose approval Henry would rather have had than that of More, the one councillor who could be guaranteed to stay on the right side of the line which divides the statesman from the yes-man. Henry took a close personal interest in the research into his divorce (the document which had presented his case to the papal tribunal in 1529 was called 'the king's book'), and with his own conscience now impregnably fortified by the arguments of Wakefield and others, Henry could not fathom how anyone of goodwill could possibly disagree with him. But to the king's growing frustration, More could not be persuaded, although he compromised his personal feelings far enough to present Henry's case formally to Parliament in 1531 in his official capacity as Lord Chancellor – though, with characteristic subtlety, he avoided reading out the king's case himself, leaving it to a royal secretary to perform what he probably found a distasteful task. Other royal scholars, following a suggestion made by Thomas Cranmer, whose career in Henry's service was now taking off, were touring the universities of Europe canvassing opinions from sympathetic theologians and lawyers. Others still were combing chronicles and archives for useful precedents and ideas, on the impossibility of summoning an English king before a tribunal outside his kingdom, on the right of a local or national Church to resolve its problems on a local basis (rather than at Rome), and on the circumstances in which papal sanctions could legitimately be ignored. It was out of these research materials that the doctrine of the 'royal supremacy' would be born – though it was far from obvious as yet that such would be the fruit.

This major research effort underpinned Henry's decision to 'go public' on the divorce. There was, not surprisingly, a great deal of public sympathy with Catherine, who looked like the stereotypical 'wronged woman'. When royal agents sought the opinion of Oxford University in 1530, they were pelted with rotten vegetables by the women of the city. Henry's infatuation with Anne Boleyn was also common knowledge by then, and she was typecast as the home-breaker. 'Burnt arse whore' was the phrase that sprang to people's lips.

Henry wanted everyone to know that his situation was not so much an instance of the eternal triangle as a personal tragedy which could engulf his entire kingdom in disaster. So the opinions of foreign universities on his cause were presented to Parliament on 30 March 1531. Published first in Latin, and later in an English translation by Thomas Cranmer, the *Determinations of the Universities* were a full statement of the royal case. Having thus prepared his people's minds, Henry now publicly separated from his wife (though for some years their relationship had been nothing but a public façade). During the summer progress, he left her at Windsor on 11 July, and never saw her again.

Catherine's friends were not slow to respond to the king's publicity blitz. However, while Henry was still anxious to be seen as the Utopian prince, taking advice from all sides and eschewing flattery – after all, Thomas More was still his Lord Chancellor – nothing written on Catherine's behalf could be printed in England. John Fisher's views had been published in 1530 – at Alcalá in Spain, in Latin, having been smuggled out of the country by Charles V's ambassador. One of the queen's chaplains, Thomas Abel, published an English treatise in her favour, the first of a handful of such books which would be printed clandestinely in the Netherlands (another of Charles V's territories). Abel's book, a masterly presentation of the queen's case, was sufficiently notorious to earn a mention in Edward Hall's chronicle, and was deeply resented by the king. Henry himself obtained a copy of the book, which he marked with infuriated annotations. His vengeful arm was long. Abel, steadfastly loyal to his queen, would be thrown into the Tower of London in 1534, emerging only to be hanged, drawn and quartered in 1540.

All the propaganda in the world, however, did not bring a solution any nearer. There were plenty of ideas around, but no policy. Early in 1531, still goading the clergy, who, he rightly suspected, were by no means solidly behind him, Henry required Convocation to recognise him as 'Supreme Head of the Church of England'. After much anxious consultation, they granted his demand, 'as far as the law of Christ allows' – a useful proviso which could mean anything or nothing. With a view to influencing the Pope, Henry reiterated his absolute refusal to have the case settled outside his dominions, and, in 1532, threatened to cut off English revenues to Rome. Meanwhile, his ministers, led by the emerging figure of Thomas Cromwell, stirred up time-honoured lay grievances against the clergy over excommunication, the powers of Church courts, and the extensive immunities of clergymen from royal courts. Even the affair of the unfortunate Richard Hunne was dragged up again. Early in 1532, Thomas Cromwell had compiled the 'Supplication against the Ordinaries', a bill of complaints against the clergy which was launched in Parliament as a 'spontaneous' petition to Henry to curtail clerical privilege and arrogance. By way of a response, Henry called upon Convocation to abandon its traditional claim to legislative autonomy and to agree that in future all its legislation should be subject to royal assent or veto. This in effect overthrew the 'liberty of the church' guaranteed by the first article of Magna Carta. When Convocation gave way and agreed on 15 May, it was too much for the Lord Chancellor. Although More's resignation next day was tactfully framed in terms of ill health, the timing made its true significance unmistakable. Thomas More could no longer reconcile service to his king with fidelity to his conscience.

The late 1520s and the early 1530s, in the political context furnished by the divorce, saw a reconfiguration of religious interest groups which jeopardised the dominance of the Catholic faith in England. Essentially, while many devotees of the traditional religion and its practices tended to sympathise with Catherine of Aragon and therefore to oppose the king, those who were attracted to the 'new learning' (as it was called) of Protestantism sensed their chance to win the king's favour and sympathy. Only one leading Protestant, William Tyndale, now a refugee abroad and rather out of touch, opposed the divorce. In a startlingly ill-informed pamphlet entitled *The Practice of Prelates*, he actually claimed that the king's 'great matter' was nothing more than a plot by nasty bishops, masterminded by Cardinal Wolsey, to confound poor Henry's conscience. The other early Protestant leaders, such as Robert Barnes, Hugh Latimer and Thomas Cranmer, shrewdly took Henry's side. Perhaps their consciences were clear, though one cannot help feeling that if Henry had been looking for permission to marry his brother's widow, rather than looking for a way out of such a marriage, both the king and his scholarly supporters would have been conscientiously convinced that the provision in Deuteronomy encouraging such marriages under certain circumstances was enough to justify what might otherwise have seemed a breach of the prohibition in Leviticus on marrying a brother's wife.

On the other hand, none of the three Englishmen who had published books against Luther in Henry's wake (Thomas More, John Fisher and an Oxford theologian named Edward Powell) felt able to support the divorce. Powell preached publicly against it, as did one of Fisher's oldest friends, Nicholas Wilson, Master of Michaelhouse (Fisher's old college at Cambridge), who had contributed a preface to the Latin edition of Fisher's 1521 sermon against Luther. Wilson had served as confessor the king, which made his refusal to support the divorce particularly damaging. The Observant Franciscans, who owed so much to the patronage of the king's father, were closer to Catherine than to Henry, and were very active in mobilising support for her and preaching in her favour. On Easter Sunday 1532, the head of the order in England, William Peto, went so far as to preach a sermon before the king in person at Greenwich, impugning his motives in seeking a divorce and suggesting that he was being misled by evil councillors. Henry tried to talk him round in a private interview afterwards, as he had done with Colet back in 1512, but found that Peto remained defiant. So he had one of his chaplains preach a reply the following Sunday. Peto himself showed shrewd common sense by fleeing the country shortly afterwards. He published two books against the divorce in Antwerp, one of them Thomas Abel's, and the other suspected (wrongly) of being Fisher's. For once the king's rage was impotent. Peto was declared guilty of treason by act of attainder in 1539, but even Henry's vengeful arm could not reach him in Rome.

Still more disturbingly, one of the most influential English religious figures of the day, a nun named Elizabeth Barton, known as the 'Holy Maid of Kent', was throwing her enormous personal charisma behind the queen's cause. Having been cured of epilepsy by the intervention of the Blessed Virgin Mary in dramatic circumstances, Elizabeth Barton was credited with miraculous and prophetic powers and became the leader of a sort of Catholic revivalist movement. The poor and middling sort flocked in thousands to see and hear her, while the rich and powerful sought her advice and intercession. Her public message, mediated through a group of scholarly monks and friars (especially the Observant Franciscans) based at religious houses in Canterbury, combined calls for moral renewal with apocalyptic warnings against the spread of Lutheran heresy, against Henry's plans to get rid of his wife, and against his encroachment on the privileges of the Church. The Holy Maid commanded a great deal of popular support. She also earned the hatred of the king.

The Holy Maid's chief impact upon the political situation in England was to stiffen the resolve of the Archbishop of Canterbury, William Warham, not to take any action prejudicial to the position of the papacy. Elizabeth Barton was a Kentishwoman by origin, and had become a nun at the convent of St Sepulchre's in Canterbury itself. It was a commission under Warham's authority which had authenticated her miraculous cure and her spiritual experiences, and he subsequently had more than one personal interview with her. Henry's great principle was that the case had to be resolved in England – which meant, in effect, by the Archbishop of Canterbury. As long as Warham was Archbishop, there was no prospect of that.

6

DELIVERING THE DIVORCE: 1533

It was Warham's death that started the countdown. The obvious choice to replace him was Stephen Gardiner, who, after a glittering career at Cambridge University, had joined Cardinal Wolsey's service in the 1520s and had then been poached by the king in 1529 to serve as his principal secretary. He had been tireless in his efforts for the divorce, and in 1531 he had been rewarded with appointment as bishop of Winchester. However, since then he had blotted his copybook. For early in 1532 he drafted the clergy's reply to the 'Supplication against the Ordinaries', a misjudgement which for a while cost him Henry's trust and favour. Gardiner was therefore passed over, and the see of Canterbury was bestowed upon the still little-known Thomas Cranmer. Cranmer had now risen far enough in royal service to be posted as Henry's ambassador to the court of Charles V, but his summons to Canterbury was a surprise to everybody – not least to him. While the imperial court was in Nuremberg, Cranmer had become attracted both to the new 'evangelical' (or Protestant) teachings of Luther and his followers, and to Margaret, the niece of the leader of the Protestant Reformation in the city, Andreas Osiander. It is not clear which attracted him first. In any case, rather rashly and, for a Catholic priest, strictly illegally, he married her. Concealing this alliance from his sovereign, who set his face firmly against allowing priests to marry, was not the least of the challenges that Cranmer faced over the next fifteen years.

By the time the news of his promotion reached him, Cranmer had accompanied Charles down to Mantua, and before he could make it back from Italy, Henry was preparing the diplomatic chessboard for the dramatic moves that he was planning. Another cross-Channel summit meeting with the king of France was arranged. It was not the Field of Cloth of Gold, and there were no wrestling matches this time – both men were a little old for such youthful high-jinks. But the meeting was far more momentous in terms of practical politics. Its most important aspect was that Henry took with him not Catherine – whom he certainly no longer considered as in any sense his wife – but Anne Boleyn, who on 1 September 1532 was made a peeress in her own right, Marchioness of Pembroke, to let her rank second only to the king in his entourage. The trip itself lasted over a month (11 October–14 November), and secured French support for a divorce and second marriage which would detach Henry from the Imperial camp. Even more importantly, it was probably on this trip that Anne finally surrendered to the king's advances. Counting backwards from her daughter's birth in early September 1533, we can see that she became pregnant shortly after the trip to France. According to one source, Henry actually married Anne secretly upon their return, on 14

November. Other sources suggest a date in January, but while the later date is generally favoured by scholars, in some ways the earlier date would fit better with what we know of Henry's curious conscience. It would have been typical of him to seek to regularise his liaison with Anne as soon as possible after she had surrendered herself to him, and the alliance with France gave him the diplomatic support he needed to take that step.

Anne's pregnancy added urgency to proceedings. Whatever else happened, the child had to be born within lawful wedlock to be capable of inheritance under English law. If to modern eyes Henry's decision to remarry before securing his divorce looks like bigamy, we must remember that he had already convinced himself that his first marriage was contrary to God's law and that he was therefore not married at all. Legally, however, the situation was far from clear, so Thomas Cromwell, emerging now as the king's chief minister, was set busy drafting the enabling legislation under which the incoming Archbishop of Canterbury would deliver the required verdict on Henry's first marriage. The resultant Act of Appeals (forbidding judicial appeals to Rome) opened with a ringing declaration:

> Where by divers sundry old histories and chronicles, it is manifestly declared and expressed, that this realm of England is an empire... governed by one supreme head and king... unto whom a body politic... ought to bear, next unto God, a natural and humble obedience...

This claim to 'imperial' status, tantamount to what we understand by 'sovereignty', was the basis on which the act maintained that no English person could lawfully be summoned to answer before any foreign jurisdiction, nor, for that matter, lawfully appeal to any such jurisdiction. It did not need to spell out the fact that the papacy was the target of this law. There was no other foreign jurisdiction to which English people at that time addressed legal petitions or appeals.

Thomas Cranmer set foot once more upon English soil early in the new year, and was consecrated Archbishop of Canterbury on 30 March 1533. The rituals included taking an oath of loyalty to the Pope, which he had no intention of keeping. On this occasion he salved his conscience by entering a written protest against the oath beforehand, though, understandably enough, this was not widely publicised. (It was not the last time he would break an oath.) Almost his first task in office was to put in place the final groundworks for the divorce. The Convocation of the clergy was presented in April with two crucial questions: whether marriage to a deceased brother's widow was forbidden in the Bible, and whether the Pope had any power to suspend this prohibition in particular cases. Three years of anticlerical agitation and fiscal pressure had done their work. The required answers (respectively, yes, and no) were given on 5 April, with only a handful of clergymen daring to defy the king. Their last-ditch resistance was led by John Fisher, who was arrested next day (Palm Sunday) to prevent him from preaching against the decisions, and was kept under house arrest until after Anne's coronation in June. This was an era when a well-judged sermon at a critical moment could provoke a riot or even a rebellion, and there had been pulpit squabbles across the realm as clergymen such as the conservative Edward Powell and the Protestant Hugh Latimer voiced their conflicting opinions on the divorce, royal policy, and the status of the new religious ideas ('the gospel'

to its supporters, new-fangled heresy to its opponents).
Archbishop Cranmer therefore imposed a general ban
on preaching in order to restore calm.

Armed with the conclusions of Convocation, and
shielded by the Act of Appeals, Cranmer summoned
Henry and Catherine before him at Dunstable on 10
May to defend the legitimacy of their marriage. The
proceedings were relatively simple, as Henry offered
no defence and Catherine refused to attend. Cranmer
annulled their marriage on 23 May and Catherine was
consigned to internal exile under the title of 'Princess
Dowager', which she refused to accept.

Henry had been unable to give Anne a splendid
wedding, but he made up for this with her coronation,
on Whit Sunday (1 June) 1533. Although the pamphlet
published to record the event insisted on the joyous
acclaim of the people, the Imperial ambassador's account
suggests at best a sullen acquiescence. The show was
spectacular, but it did not win people over. Nor was
the coronation an overwhelming success among the
aristocracy. Even some peers failed to attend, most
notably George Talbot, Earl of Shrewsbury, one of the
king's oldest and closest companions (who was represented,
in his absence, by his son). Thomas More was deliberately
provocative about it. Some of his clerical friends clubbed
together and sent him £20 to buy some new clothes
and make his peace with the king by turning up to the
coronation. He refused their invitation but took their
money anyway! A satisfying gesture, no doubt, but perhaps
for once his taste for a sharp jest betrayed him. The joke was
hardly calculated to soften Henry's heart towards him.

Catherine was not short of friends abroad, however,
and her appeal was pressed at Rome, where, in September,
the Pope adjudged her marriage to Henry valid, and

began to take sanctions against Henry for divorcing her. As Anne had now borne Henry's child (disappointingly for him, another daughter, Elizabeth), it was essential to safeguard the claim to the throne of that child, and of any further offspring. In the meantime, there was also unfinished business with the Holy Maid of Kent. She was arrested in September, interrogated, and put under pressure to acknowledge herself a fraud. What precisely she admitted is unclear. It was claimed that she did indeed admit to being a fraud, but there is no formal legal record of such a confession, and it sits rather ill with her ultimate fate. That autumn Henry convened a Great Council (a sort of augmented version of the normal King's Council, strengthened by most of the spiritual and temporal peers as well as by other prominent figures) to consider, among other things, how to handle the Maid. The outcome was clear. She had predicted, according to one version of her prophecies, that if Henry divorced Catherine, he would lose his throne within six months. Six months to the day (was there an element of caution as well as of showmanship in the timing?) since Cranmer had annulled that marriage, Elizabeth Barton was compelled to stand outside St Paul's Cathedral doing penance while a preacher detailed her offences and proclaimed her guilty by her own admission. Yet she was never put on trial, and no evidence against her was ever produced. It is not the historian's task to decide whether she was inspired or deluded. But she was probably sincere. Whatever the truth, the spectacle outside St Paul's discredited her totally. Two books of the Maid's prophecies were printed in her heyday. Henry's government banned them so effectively that not a single copy of either of them survives.

7

THE BREAK WITH ROME: 1534 - 1535

Given the Pope's decision to act against Henry, it was essential to undermine and perhaps terminate papal authority in England. At a meeting of the king's council in December 1533, it was decided that henceforward the Pope would be known in England as 'the bishop of Rome', a change in style which obviously belittled papal claims. It is from about this time that imperial motifs become prevalent in Henry's public documents and official propaganda. The traditional descriptions of the king as 'his highness' and 'his grace' start to be joined by the new formula 'his majesty': 'majesty' was the quality which Roman law attributed to the person and office of the emperor. Hitherto it had been rare in English, and almost unknown in official documents. Appearing for the first time in statutes and proclamations in 1534, 'his majesty' became first common and eventually normative.

The king's vengeance against the Holy Maid of Kent did not end with public disgrace and humiliation. Early in 1534, an act of attainder was drawn up to condemn her and her supporters for treason. Acts of attainder were statutes hitherto used to confirm the guilt and punishments of notorious traitors – those who had borne arms against the king or who had been convicted of treason in a court of law. However, Thomas Cromwell used them to shortcut due process, simply declaring people guilty of treason and liable to its punishments without the trouble and expense of a trial. Henry was out to make a clean sweep of his opponents. While only a couple of Observant Franciscans were included in the act of attainder, the order as a whole found itself facing Henry's fury. In effect, the English Observant Franciscans were closed down. Their houses were handed either to the ordinary Franciscans or to the Austin Friars, and many of their members fled the country rather than accept their transfer to another rule.

Henry also sought to use the act of attainder against his two most prominent opponents. John Fisher of Rochester was included in the bill on the grounds that he had met the Maid and listened to her prophecies without reporting them to the king, an omission here interpreted as 'misprision' (that is, concealment) of treason. His defence was perfectly reasonable. He pleaded not only that her prophecies were public knowledge, but also that he knew she had actually met the king and told him of her visions face to face. Oddly enough, this was true. The records of expenditure from the king's 'privy purse' survive for a few years around 1530, and one of the payments made, on 1 February 1530, was a handsome £2 given to two nuns from Canterbury 'by way of the king's gracious reward'. This can only have been to the Holy Maid, who was no doubt travelling with a companion (members of religious orders away from their houses were meant to travel in pairs). But this was not enough to persuade the House of Lords to risk royal displeasure by exempting him from the act. Thomas More was luckier. Canny lawyer that he was, he had been careful to keep the Holy Maid at arm's length when she came to see him, refusing to hear anything about her prophecies. This really was a powerful defence, and the Lords accepted it, removing his name from the bill. Henry was furious, and wanted to go down to Parliament and browbeat the Lords into putting More's name back in, but his councillors, led by More's successor as Lord Chancellor, Thomas Audley, talked him out of it, convincing him that even a personal appearance would not secure More's condemnation, and that the consequent loss of face would be a political catastrophe.

Thomas More had escaped, but not for long. The net began to close with the next major piece of legislation, the Act of Succession, which enshrined in English law the recent alterations in the king's matrimonial arrangements, and required every adult English male to uphold them by swearing a personal oath to the contents of the act. In this extraordinary requirement we can for a moment see what is otherwise concealed from us by the fulsome words of flattering chroniclers and the pompous pleonasms of statutes – the very real nervousness of a king who, driven on by urgent personal and dynastic necessities, was pursuing a revolutionary and plainly unpopular policy. The oath, which included statements prejudicial to papal primacy, was at first administered to select groups: the peers, members of Parliament, courtiers and royal servants. On Friday 17 April it was offered to the clergy of London, and met with a handful of recalcitrants. John Fisher refused it, as did

Thomas More, who was called in with the clergy. They were promptly thrown into the Tower. The following Monday, the oath was put before a wider public: the people of London. Nobody refused it. Compliance may have been fostered by the spectacle of the Holy Maid and a handful of her closest associates being dragged that morning through the streets of the city to Tyburn (roughly where Marble Arch now stands), hanged, cut down and then cut up, before being displayed in crudely butchered pieces on the gates of the city and London Bridge. The man who did this ghastly work, 'a cunning butcher in quartering of men', was himself hanged a few years later for robbery.

Henry's general worries about his own people, whose sympathy for Catherine of Aragon was clear, were accompanied by more specific concerns about powerful noblemen in his domains and the power of the Emperor abroad. The spring of 1534 saw him summon to London the two men who might do most to threaten his position: the Earl of Kildare, the most powerful man in Ireland, and at this point the king's appointed lieutenant governing it; and Lord Dacre, the Warden of the Marches, exercising the king's authority in the far north of England and the man primarily responsible for protecting the kingdom against the Scots. At the same time, he despatched a new and vigorous agent to impose law and order on the traditionally violent and disorderly Welsh Marches, where English government merged into the less clearly defined jurisdictions and social systems of Wales. The general Tudor preoccupation with these three regions (Ireland, Wales and the north) derived chiefly from the fact that they tended to provide so much of the manpower in times of civil war. If there was going to be an internal threat to Henry's regime, it would have to involve one or more of these regions. The governmental interventions of early 1534 were pre-emptive strikes against potential centres of opposition.

Ironically, one of these interventions provoked the very crisis it was trying to pre-empt. The Earl of Kildare's son, Thomas Fitzgerald (known as 'Silken Thomas'), fearing, probably rightly, that his father's summons to London and imprisonment in the Tower heralded a general assault on their family's pre-eminent position in Ireland, raised his standard against Henry VIII. Appealing to the Emperor and the Pope for assistance, he put himself forward as a defender of the Church, beginning the process by which the Catholic faith and incipient Irish nationalism would combine to form a powerful ideology of opposition to English rule. It took Henry's forces two years to restore to Ireland the approximation to peace which generally prevailed there, and much of the rest of the reign was taken up with efforts to extend and strengthen direct royal authority in the island.

The other interventions were more successful. The reign of terror which was implemented in the Welsh Marches by Rowland Lee, Bishop of Coventry and Lichfield, went down in bardic literature as a legendary time of implacable and draconian justice, and paved the way for the full integration of Wales itself into the kingdom of England from 1536, when the English system of shires, justices of the peace, and representation in Parliament began to be extended to that whole region. Yet perhaps the biggest lesson of the developments in Wales was that they were implemented not by some great peer or magnate but by a bishop, whose political power was derived entirely from office under the Crown. The last major Welsh magnates, the Duke of Buckingham and Rhys ap Griffith, had both been destroyed in the 1520s.

The new regime for Wales fostered the emergence there of a gentry class which, as in so much of the English south-east, would look directly to the king for protection and preferment, rather than to traditional baronial intermediaries.

Lord Dacre was put on trial for treason before his peers. The charges were piffling, and mostly revolved around the negotiations with the Scots which any Warden of the Marches had to keep up if a reasonable degree of stability was to be achieved in the frontier zone. He secured an acquittal, a very rare achievement in the annals of Tudor treason trials. The fact that Dacre's defence proved convincing shows how gingerly the king had to tread at this time. Not that vindication meant that he kept his job. Henry replaced him anyway, and still mulcted him in £10,000. Later Catholic lore handed down a tale that Henry brought Dacre down for fear that he might lead opposition to royal policy in the House of Lords. And it was also rumoured that once Henry had broken with Rome and established the royal supremacy, he asked Dacre what he thought about it, only to receive this reply: 'Hereafter, then, when Your Majesty offendeth, you may absolve yourself.' It is of course unlikely that Lord Dacre dared address his sovereign in such an insolent fashion, but the story may well give us a sense of what a typical Catholic peer really thought of Henry's proceedings. But whatever Dacre thought, Henry had achieved his immediate objective. Although the north was to prove less amenable to Henrician reform than Wales, for now, in 1534, all was quiet.

The Act of Succession of 1534 was not the end of the road. When Parliament reconvened in autumn, it was presented with a still more radical bill to establish the 'royal supremacy' over the Church of England, removing England entirely from the jurisdiction of the Pope, whose authority had been under open attack in England for about a year. More than any of the previous acts, this was seen to be a point of no return. Stephen Gardiner, who voted as a bishop in the House of Lords when the bill was passed, was to recall twenty years later that Parliament 'was with most great cruelty constrained to abolish and put away the primacy from the bishop of Rome'. Henry's supreme headship, 'under Christ' but otherwise without any qualification or restriction, represented the apotheosis of Henry as royal theologian. He was now not only emperor in his own kingdom, but Pope as well. The act was carefully phrased to make it clear that Parliament was recognising a power which already belonged by right to the king, rather than claiming to confer a new power upon him. Various acts in 1534 and 1535 invested him with power to appoint bishops (rather than simply nominate them to the Pope), to reform canon law (although this was never achieved!) and to collect for himself the traditional taxes paid to the Pope (taxes he collected more effectively than any Pope had ever done). Indeed, by an act passed many years later – one which did little more than recognise what was by then political reality – Henry was personally granted the power to define the doctrine of his Church and to amend it as he saw fit. True, he never actually exercised this power, but in theory it gave him powers exceeding even that of papal infallibility. The armchair theologian of the 1520s now sat in the 'cathedra' of the Pope, and was happy, from time to time, to appear in public in this welcome guise.

In the meantime, Henry found that there some marvellous fringe benefits to his new status. He knew, for example, of a stunning gold crucifix in the treasury of St Paul's Cathedral, studded with diamonds, rubies, emeralds, and pearls. In May 1535 he sent a message to the canons of the cathedral asking them to bring it to Court for him to see. They took the hint with pleasing rapidity, and sent it along with the message that they offered it as a free gift to their good lord the king.

So attached was Henry from the start to his new title that supporting legislation rapidly followed making it treason to deny his right to it. This, too, caused problems in Parliament, as it was generally seen as making mere words a matter of treason. The Commons managed to insert what they thought was a limiting clause restricting the penalties of treason to those who would 'maliciously' deny the king's supremacy. It was a hollow victory. In the summer of 1535, Thomas More, John Fisher and a handful of Carthusian monks were charged in a series of trials with denying the supremacy. The Carthusians had mostly volunteered their opinions. A simple subterfuge induced Fisher to offer his. He was told that the king really wanted to know his honest opinion, privately, in order to help him guide his own conscience on the issue. The bishop in him could not resist this appeal to his pastoral instincts, and he spoke his mind. At his trial, Fisher's defence was that his denial of the supremacy was not malicious. The judges, however, ruled that the adverb 'maliciously' was describing, rather than qualifying, the action: any denial of the supremacy, they concluded, was by definition malicious. Fisher was convicted easily. Thomas More, as usual, had been much more cautious, and defended himself adroitly in court. His conviction was secured on the testimony, probably perjured, of a single man, Richard Rich. It is of course possible, as some historians seem to think, that Thomas

More lied in denying what Rich affirmed. Yet More's defence remains compelling: if he thought so little of oaths as to perjure himself in court, why he should he have baulked at taking oaths to the succession and the supremacy when, even at this late hour, submission would have restored him to favour and fortune?

The victims went to their deaths at intervals from May to July. The Carthusians were treated to the full barbarity of hanging, drawing and quartering. Fisher and More enjoyed the dubious mercy of the king who had once been their friend, and were beheaded. The Pope had endeavoured to extend some protection to Fisher by appointing him to the college of cardinals, hoping that even Henry might think twice about executing a Prince of the Church. But when news reached the king of this offer of a 'red hat', Henry quipped that he would have to wear it on his shoulders. It was Thomas More whom Henry most desperately wanted to win over, and the other executions were spread over the preceding months in order to help him change his mind. More's execution was the culmination of the butcheries of 1535, and Henry is said to have attended in disguise: it is not every king who gets to execute quite literally his most famous subject. More's scaffold joke about his beard (he asked the headsman to be careful not to cut it, as it had done nothing to offend the king) apparently led Henry to shave off the beard he had sported for years, and go clean-shaven.

The executions of dissidents were part of a twofold strategy of enforcement. The other main thrust was through propaganda, to some extent in print, but even more by the main mass medium of what was still a predominantly oral rather than literate culture – the sermon. The systematic way in which the new theory of royal supremacy over the Church was promulgated is, again, testimony to the clear-headedness of Henry and his ministers about what it was they were doing. The propaganda campaign was certainly unprecedented in English history, in volume and orchestration. Printed books also played their part. The intellectual underpinnings of the Act of Supremacy, the collection of proof texts assembled by Henry's scholars over the preceding four or five years, were drawn together and published as *De vera differentia* (*The True Difference between Royal and Ecclesiastical Power*). Its target audience was probably the clergyman who might be putting together his own sermon on the subject and needed a handy source of material. A more polished and literary presentation of Henry's position was Stephen Gardiner's treatise *De vera obedientia* (*On True Obedience*). Another Latin publication, it was written more for the benefit of a learned readership in Europe than for that of the English people, and copies were sent abroad to foreign princes. It was also designed to restore Gardiner to royal favour. In this regard its success was mixed. He was rewarded with appointment as ambassador to the court of the French king. This was prestigious (as well as onerous), but probably also represented an easy way for Thomas Cromwell to keep his main potential rival at a safe distance.

8

GOD'S WORD & HENRY'S REFORMATION: JANUARY - SEPTEMBER 1536

Those who shouted loudest in the chorus of denunciation of the Pope were those who had already begun to lean towards the 'evangelical' Protestant teachings coming into the country from Germany and Switzerland. As far as Protestants were concerned, the papacy had already revealed itself to be the Antichrist by its resolute condemnation of their key doctrine, 'justification by faith alone'. The fiery rhetoric ignited by this identification of the Pope as the sworn enemy of Christ and devotee of the devil was extremely useful to Henry, who privately inclined towards this view himself, even though he was as hostile as the Pope to justification by faith alone. He was more than happy to let his preachers off the leash with this idea, and Archbishop Cranmer himself set the trend on Sunday 6 February 1536 with a two-hour tirade denouncing the papal Antichrist. Henry's official publications never invoked the 'papal Antichrist', but the concept was heavily used in the sort of 'arm's length' propaganda issued by royal supporters such as Richard Morison.

Preachers galore jumped on the bandwagon. Heartfelt denunciation of the papacy became for a while the passport to success. From 1534 to 1536, the men whom Henry appointed as bishops in his Church were all drawn from the ranks of the evangelicals. This reflects the influence of his new wife, Anne, who had herself been interested in the persons and the writings of the Protestant reformers since the late 1520s. As early as 1528 she had written to Cardinal Wolsey appealing for clemency for a London parish priest, Dr Thomas Farman, the rector of All Hallows Honey Lane, who was in prison under suspicion of Lutheranism. The suspicions were well founded. Farman's curate, Thomas Garrett, had been selling Lutheran and other Protestant books in both Oxford and Cambridge, and Farman himself, under interrogation, unmistakably affirmed the Lutheran doctrine of justification. That Anne should have been interceding on his behalf speaks volumes about the path of her religious development. Her own taste in literature is equally revealing. Her personal library included a number of French evangelical texts, some of them translations of Protestant works from German.

The best known of the new bishops of the mid-1530s, Hugh Latimer, Nicholas Shaxton and William Barlow, had all been chaplains in Anne's service before their promotion. These men in particular, and the evangelical preachers in general, eagerly stretched their new freedom to its utmost, and did as much as they dared to advance their broader Protestant agenda under the cover of establishing the supremacy. Given that many of these men were preaching regularly in the presence of the king, it is hardly to be thought that he was oblivious to their little game. But he probably reckoned he could control the pace of change, and was prepared to pay the price for some talented and unequivocal pulpit support for the supremacy.

Some of these preachers, though, were little enough to the king's doctrinal taste. Thomas Cranmer licensed various men to preach anywhere in the kingdom. One of them was the same Thomas Garrett who had been peddling forbidden books in the 1520s. A few years later he would go to the stake for his Lutheran beliefs. Another was Thomas Swynnerton, a man who had studied at Luther's feet in Wittenberg. Robert Barnes, a fugitive heretic in the late 1520s, and another who had made his way to Wittenberg, was now on the fringes of the king's council, a close confidant of Thomas Cromwell, and employed in the diplomatic approaches to the German princes that started around this time. He went to the stake with Garrett in 1540. But in 1535 such men were in high favour thanks to their anti-papal zeal.

It was not only the Protestants who preached the supremacy, though. Conservative clergy, and especially bishops, were expected to show where their true loyalties lay. John Stokesley of London, Cuthbert Tunstall of Durham, John Longland of Lincoln and many lesser figures had to perform at court or at Paul's Cross, publicly committing themselves to the new orthodoxy. At every level of the Church, the message was controlled and pumped out. In June 1535 every parish priest in the country was instructed to preach the royal supremacy to his flock week in, week out; this obligation was reduced a year or so later to preaching on the subject at least twice every three months. The intensity of this preaching campaign reflected not only Henry's nervousness about the reception of the new doctrine, but also the nature of his commitment to it. He did not just like to be obeyed: he liked to be right. It was not enough for him that people accept the supremacy or even that they swear to it (an explicit oath was in fact required only of clergymen). He wanted them to believe in it sincerely and without any reservation.

From this time on, the royal supremacy was at the heart of Henry's religious sensibility. As usual with him, the expedient became a matter of conscience, so much so that we should think of his adoption of the royal supremacy not as a cynical ruse, but as a kind of religious conversion. He spoke of it in theological, almost mystical terms. For him, the supremacy was 'the Word of God'. His subjects swiftly adapted to the new habits of thought and speech he required of them, and learned what he liked to hear. Henry Parker, Lord Morley, an old-fashioned aristocrat who often bestowed upon his sovereign the fruits of his limited literary skills, offered him these thoughts in a pamphlet published in 1539:

> Blessed mayest thou be called, Most Christian King Henry the VIII, Supreme Head of the Church of England. Blessed art thou, whom God hath taught to spy out the perilous doctrine of the Bishop of Rome, whereby the people of England are brought from darkness to light, from error to the highway of right knowledge, from danger of death eternal to life that never endeth, to be short, even from Hell to Heaven.

Henry was 'evangelical' about it, and spoke of opening the eyes of his fellow princes to this truth. He fully expected to lead an international movement of princes against the Pope, and opened negotiations with the Schmalkaldic League with a view to this. Unfortunately, the committed Lutheranism of the German princes was, in the end, too much for him to swallow, although his own evangelical advisers, such as Cromwell and Cranmer, did their very best to sugar the pill and tickle it down his throat. When the negotiations finally broke down, in 1538, it was largely because Henry himself looked at what the League was saying about the Mass – the focus of his own attack on Luther back in 1521 – and refused to make any compromise with them. Compromise, for him, meant other people adjusting to his views. When it became apparent that the Schmalkaldic princes were not moving, he simply gave up on them. There was to be no future in England for what Henry always regarded as 'the damnable heresy of the Lutheran sect'.

Henry's personal commitment to the royal supremacy explains why the expedient so triumphantly survived, in 1536, the rapid unravelling of the complex web of circumstances which had given rise to it. At the start of the year Catherine of Aragon died, doubtless of natural causes (albeit hastened by grief and ill treatment) rather than from the poison of which rumour was soon whispering. Notoriously, Henry's hatred pursued her beyond the grave. On hearing the news of her death, he donned ludicrously loud yellow clothing, rather than the sober costume which would normally be worn to mark the death of a princess. Catherine's corpse was consigned for burial to Peterborough Abbey, and there were no obsequies at Court or in London. Soon afterwards, Anne Boleyn lost a child through a miscarriage. Rumour was swift to detect in this the judgement of divine providence on her and her husband. In any case, her failure to bear the king a son after three years of marriage may have weakened her hold upon his affections. Within a few months, she would follow Catherine to disgrace and the grave.

The fall of Anne Boleyn was sudden and dramatic. While Henry VIII was sitting and watching May Day jousts at Greenwich, a message was brought to him which caused him to leave the festivities abruptly and grimly. That message purported to bring proof of accusations that Anne was guilty of adultery (a treasonable offence in a queen) which had first been brought to the king's attention a day or two before. Historians still disagree about the truth or falsehood of the allegations (though the consensus is that they were false). But Henry called for an investigation, and rapidly became convinced that they were true. Suspicion ran through the court like ripples in a pond, and some of the king's closest friends were implicated, most notably Sir Henry Norris, the Groom of the Stool and thus the head of Henry's Privy Chamber, responsible for attending on the king's person. Another victim was George Boleyn, Viscount Rochford, Anne's own brother – with whom she was accused of conducting an incestuous affair which not even historians unsympathetic to her claims of innocence tend to credit. Norris and Rochford had been the leading riders in the jousts which Henry left in rage. Anne was arrested the next day, and was tried and executed, like her alleged lovers, within three weeks.

Henry might have been less receptive to the charges against Anne had his eye not already fallen upon a pretty young girl at court, Jane Seymour. His infatuation with her was common knowledge around the court in March. Henry lost no time. On 20 May 1536, the day after Anne's execution, Henry and Jane were betrothed. The wedding took place ten days later in York Place (or 'Whitehall'), a palace Henry had acquired after Wolsey's fall. A new Act of Succession soon undid the provisions of its predecessor of 1534, conferring upon Henry, in the absence of heirs by Jane, the power to determine the succession by letters patent or even in his will.

The disappearance from the scene of both Catherine of Aragon and Anne Boleyn might have cleared the way for a reconciliation with Rome. This was certainly how Stephen Gardiner saw things from the distant vantage-point of the French court, where he was Henry's ambassador, and he even started putting out unofficial feelers towards papal diplomats there. Gardiner, however, had read the signals wrongly, and received no encouragement from home. He was fortunate that no word of his dealings came to Henry's ears, as such contacts could very easily have been construed as treason and employed to terminate his career.

But reconciliation of a different kind was afoot. Implicated in her mother's disgrace, Mary Tudor had remained loyal to her mother as long as she lived. Now, though, deprived of her mother's support and perhaps heartened by the sudden elimination of her mother's rival, Anne Boleyn, she was at last induced to conform to her father's will and make her peace with him. Following Thomas Cromwell's helpful advice, she subscribed to the royal supremacy, the repudiation of the papacy, and the 'incestuous and unlawful' nature of her parents' marriage. Even so, the price of her forgiveness was high. Her rehabilitation was completed only when Henry deigned to receive from her a letter couched in terms of repentance and humility befitting an address to the Deity:

> Most humbly prostrate before the feet of your most excellent Majesty, your most humble, faithful and obedient subject, which hath so extremely offended your most gracious Highness, that mine heavy and

fearful heart dare not presume to call you father, nor
Your Majesty hath any cause by my deserts, saving the
benignity of your most blessed nature doth surmount
all evils, offences, and trespasses, and is ever merciful
and ready to accept the penitent calling for grace, in any
convenient time...

Mary's self-abasement secured her return to court and
favour – and may even have saved her life. Though
the stigma of illegitimacy remained, she would in due
course regain her place in the line of succession. In the
meantime, her position at Court was consolidated by
the good relationship she struck up with Henry's new
bride, Jane Seymour. They were much the same age, and
shared a conservative taste in religious devotion.

In the meantime, led by Cromwell and Cranmer,
the 'evangelicals' continued to make all the running
in the Church of England and sowed the seeds of
religious change, partly by spreading Protestant ideas
at the grass roots (though real Protestants remained
in a distinct minority), but more importantly by
persuading the king himself to take tentative steps
towards a thorough reformation. Three major
religious policies were sold to the king during
the three years following the executions of Fisher
and More: the dissolution of the monasteries, the
abolition of pilgrimages and associated practices,
and the publication of the Bible in English. Henry
took some convincing over the first two, but had
always had some sympathy for the third.

If almost anyone in England in 1535 had been told
that within five years every monastery, convent and
friary in the kingdom would have been closed down
and their vast assets transferred to the king, they
would never have believed it. Looking back at the

process, and especially at its sheer speed, it is easy to conclude that it was the product of some master plan. Cardinal Pole later claimed that Thomas Cromwell had bought Henry VIII's favour by promising to make him richer than any previous king of England. Henry himself, looking back from the vantage point of the 1540s, credited himself with extraordinary sagacity and subtlety in implementing a grand plan to close down the monasteries. Yet the story looks very different when seen from the front rather than the back.

The valuation of all Church property which the government organised in 1535 was not undertaken with a view to expropriating the Church, but in order to tax it more effectively now that all Church taxes went to the Crown. Nor even was the visitation of all the monasteries in late 1535 and early 1536 begun in order to gather material to discredit monks and thus smooth the way for the dissolution. Its primary purpose was to ensure that every single monk and nun in England signed up, literally, to the royal supremacy. The monasteries were still institutions of immense power and influence, and under the right circumstances might have become centres of opposition to royal policy. The visitation was a demand for submission, and the intrusive moral enquiries which formed part of the visitation's agenda were probably akin to the anticlerical agitation fomented since 1529, a means of undermining the moral authority of the monasteries: a sort of insurance policy. It was in the context of the salacious gossip that some of the visitors collected that the idea of closing down monasteries on moral grounds seems to have emerged.

The outcome was the first act for the suppression of monasteries (1536), which declared that, unless specifically spared by the king, all religious houses whose gross income was less than £200 a year would be taken into the king's hands, and their occupants either rehoused in other monasteries or else released from their vows to live as priests in the world. Despite the lurid tales which were paraded before members of Parliament, this act went out of its way to praise the moral standards of the larger and wealthier religious houses. This concession, combined with the fact that many poorer houses were in fact spared (usually at some considerable cost in fines and sweeteners) and that all who wished to remain in the religious life were allowed to do so, casts doubt on the idea that, at this point, Henry envisaged the complete abolition of the religious life.

Even more decisive evidence to the contrary comes from the fact that Henry himself actually refounded two religious houses – one of monks, the other of nuns – out of the proceeds of this first plunder. Bisham Abbey and the nunnery of Stixwold were re-endowed, re-staffed, and renamed after Henry VIII himself. It might perhaps have been a blind. But it would be unlike Henry to play with large sums of money and to take his own name in vain. The declared aim of these two new monasteries was to pray for the welfare in life and the eternal rest after death of himself, of his new wife, Queen Jane Seymour, and of their heirs and ancestors. There is no particular reason to disbelieve him. Indeed, the foundations probably reflected not only his affection for her but also her influence over him. Towards the end of 1536, when the Pilgrimage of Grace broke out, Jane actually begged Henry to spare the monasteries. And in the course of that summer they appeared together in a grand devotional procession on the feast of Corpus Christi (15 June), one of the most emphatically anti-Protestant gestures imaginable. Archbishops, bishops, abbots, dukes, peers and judges joined the royal couple as they proceeded to Westminster, where Mass was sung by the Dean of the Chapel Royal (and highly skilled musician), Richard Sampson, who had just been consecrated Bishop of Chichester. Jane would certainly have appreciated the signal honour of having a monastery and a nunnery established specifically for her.

The other religious policies first emerged clearly that same year, 1536, and were similarly tentative. Thomas Cromwell secured from the king a grant making him the king's 'vicegerent' (or deputy) in all spiritual and ecclesiastical matters. Armed with viceregal powers in the Church, Cromwell pursued a modestly evangelical agenda, hand in glove with Thomas Cranmer, and much to the dismay of the conservative majority of the clergy. Pulpit disputes became commonplace as theological rivals at every level dismissed each other as 'papists' or 'newfangled fellows'. Things came to a head at the meeting of Convocation (the representative body of the clergy) in the summer, when both wings of Henry's Church of England sought to make their point. Cromwell made the first move, sending one of his minions, Dr William Petre, a lawyer and not even a priest, to claim the chairmanship of the gathering as the appointed deputy of the king's Vicegerent. This amounted to a fresh assertion of lay supremacy over the clergy, an emphatic and even more obnoxious affirmation of the principle inherent in the royal supremacy. The task of delivering the keynote opening sermon was entrusted to one of the most prominent evangelical bishops, Hugh Latimer. The selection of Latimer was deliberately provocative. In the early 1530s, Convocation had twice instituted proceedings against him on charges of heresy, though he had been protected from their wrath thanks to his zealous support of Henry over the divorce. He relished this opportunity to lay down the law to his former persecutors, delivering a call for reform of an unmistakably Protestant hue. Where reformist Catholics generally maintained that the doctrine of the Church was reliable, and that reform meant bringing the defective life of the Church into line with the perfection of her doctrine, the classic Protestant analysis, at least in the early days, was to argue that the reason the moral and spiritual life of the Church was so defective was that the doctrine of the Church was corrupt and unbiblical.

The mainly conservative representatives of the various dioceses compiled a huge list of erroneous doctrines, the 'mala dogmata', which they wished to see condemned, while Cromwell and Cranmer, with a few allies such as Hugh Latimer among the bishops, sought to impose unwelcome religious changes upon them. With the king's blessing, Cromwell and Cranmer backed a statement of faith, the Ten Articles, drafted by another ally, Bishop Edward Fox of Hereford, in an attempt to resolve the divisions at Convocation, to foreclose on public disputes and debates over doctrine, and to do so in a way which smuggled in as much quasi-Protestant thinking and terminology as possible. This caused such dissension that it had to be referred to Henry VIII himself for final adjudication. Perhaps thanks to the influence of some powerful conservative clergymen close to the king, chief among them Richard Sampson, whose influence with Henry was at its zenith that summer, the Ten Articles as they finally appeared over the king's name were much less radical than they had been to start with. While Lutheran buzzwords gave away the origins of the draft, subtle modifications or additions of words and phrases blunted any radical edge in the articles concerned with doctrine. Later articles, concerned with devotional practices such as pilgrimages and prayer to the saints, criticised them in terms of superstition, abuse and excess, but without laying an axe to the trunk of popular religion. The most important feature of the document, in fact, was precisely that it was not simply issued in the name of the king, but phrased as though delivered by him in person. It depended for its authority neither on Convocation, nor on Parliament, nor indeed on the Bible, but purely upon the royal supremacy. However many hands had meddled in the drafting, the Ten Articles spoke with the king's voice.

Cromwell was able to put something of the radical edge back onto the Articles by means of his 'Injunctions' (i.e. instructions) issued to all the clergy of England later that summer. In particular, the Injunctions actively discouraged pilgrimages, the veneration of relics, and the reporting of miracles performed by saints – a complex of beliefs and practices which, often summed up as 'the cult of the saints', was of central importance in the religion of the people. He also instructed parishes to buy a copy of the Bible in English – reversing a prohibition of more than a century's standing. In fact, as only one edition of the English Bible had been printed so far (and abroad at that), and he did not say who was to pay (parish priest or parishioners), this instruction was almost universally ignored. But the very issuing of the instruction was a blow to those conservative clergymen who saw 'English books' (from which most of the 'mala dogmata' had been drawn) as the source of all evil. More importantly still, it unmistakably aligned Cromwell, who issued the Injunctions in his own name, on the basis of the authority committed to him by the king, with the movement of religious innovation. Indeed, one of the foremost members of that movement, William Tyndale, who had translated the New Testament into English, was burned for heresy in the Netherlands that same summer. The message could not have been clearer. Cromwell was on Tyndale's side.

9

THE PILGRIMAGE OF GRACE: OCTOBER - DECEMBER 1536

The religious policies of 1536 provoked the great crisis of Henry's reign, the Pilgrimage of Grace, the greatest rebellion ever faced by a Tudor monarch, and in the whole of English history second only to the Peasants' Revolt of 1381 as a popular uprising. The rising started in the context of the visitation of the churches of northern Lincolnshire by Church commissioners implementing Cromwell's Injunctions in September. This visitation, combined with a tour by other commissioners collecting a tax and with the beginning of the dissolution of the monasteries, fuelled apocalyptic rumours about government plans to strip parish churches bare and close down most of what people knew as their religious life. These fears of spiritual and material impoverishment were a potent mixture, and the spark was an inflammatory sermon denouncing the rumoured changes, which was preached on Sunday 1 October 1536 by the local vicar, Thomas Kendall, in the great parish church of Louth, the administrative centre of the region, where clergymen and local notables from miles around had gathered for the visitation. Within days Lincolnshire was up in arms. Henry VIII reacted vigorously and furiously. A proclamation denouncing the disobedience of the rebels was circulated, and troops were rapidly called up under the command of the Duke of Suffolk. As this royal army marched on Lincoln, the rebels quickly calmed down, and were dispersed with some easy promises of amnesty.

All seemed well, and the royal army itself started to disperse. But then it became apparent that, beyond the fog of events in Lincolnshire, still worse things were afoot in the north. While the government had focused its attention on Lincolnshire, revolt had spread like wildfire through the six counties of northern England. Popular and clerical risings recruited the support of the gentry and even of some peers, notably Lord Darcy. The unlikely leader of the whole movement was a minor Yorkshire gentleman named Robert Aske. A rebel force, organised as though it was an army, concentrated around the royal castle of Pontefract, which became its headquarters. It was, in effect, the English army of the north, for the most part led by the same families, and often by the same individuals, who had commanded the English forces against the Scots at Flodden Field in 1513. Adopting as its badge the Five Wounds of Christ (the wounds he received at the crucifixion) and calling itself, in the solemn oath which bound together its adherents, the 'Pilgrimage of Grace for the Commonweal', it looked remarkably like a crusade (usually defined among historians as 'an armed pilgrimage'). With other large rebel groups gathered at Carlisle and elsewhere, almost all England north of the Trent was under the control of the Pilgrims through the autumn of 1536. Their grievances were voiced at a representative assembly, and were consolidated into a list of demands which began with a call for reconciliation with Rome, went on with the reversal of recent religious changes and the restoration of suppressed monasteries, included a number of material demands relating to taxation and land law and, most threateningly, emphasised the need to eliminate the king's 'low-born' councillors, who were tactfully blamed for everything the Pilgrims hated. Foremost among these villains was of course Thomas Cromwell, but Cranmer and Latimer were not far behind in the rebel demonology.

We learn a great deal about Henry from the way he dealt with this broad-based challenge to his entire regime. The idea of resorting to concessions or compromise was inconceivable for him. His young wife, Jane, made her only venture into politics at this moment, begging Henry on bended knee to reverse his policy towards the monasteries. Henry pulled her roughly to her feet and warned her not to meddle in things which were not her concern, reminding her of the fate of her predecessor. Instead of holding out the prospect of concessions, Henry launched against the northern rebels a proclamation still sterner than that issued for Lincolnshire, and his instructions to the Duke of Norfolk were for direct military action and dire vengeance. The Pilgrims actually reopened some of the monasteries suppressed earlier that year, and Henry took this as a particular affront. He ordered Norfolk to hang some of the offending monks from the steeple of their own church. What irritated Henry more than anything was the presumption of the Pilgrims in telling him whom he should or should not have on his Privy Council. He told them in no uncertain terms that nobility was what he wanted it to be, that if he chose someone for his council that was a greater honour than any inherited rank, and that in any case his council had an ample supply of the well-born nobles whom the rebels claimed it lacked: and with men like Norfolk, Suffolk and Shrewsbury among his councillors, he had a point – although of course everybody, including the rebels, knew that Cromwell mattered more on the council than all the others put together.

Had it not been for the tactful diplomacy of the Duke of Norfolk on the ground in Yorkshire, Henry's personal intransigence might have cost him his throne. For if Norfolk had followed early royal instructions and given battle to the rebels with his inferior force, he might have been cut to pieces, in which case the road south would have lain open to a force which had tasted blood, gone too far to consider retreat, and learned that the king would not listen. In the event, Norfolk persuaded the king that negotiation was the only realistic policy, although even the non-committal concessions which he offered were probably more than Henry would have liked him to make. He guaranteed them a full and free pardon if they dispersed, and promised that the king would listen to their grievances. The fact that they believed him helps us to understand the success of the English Reformation in particular, and of the Tudor regime in general. The Pilgrims were convinced that Henry was essentially one of them, conservative in religion and politics alike, and they were thoroughly indoctrinated with the ideology of monarchy, which had long been ingrained into the English mind by the common law and the Church, and which the Tudors, trading heavily on the memory of the uncertainties of the Wars of the Roses, had made indispensable to the general sense of the viability of the social order. The fact was that Henry himself was

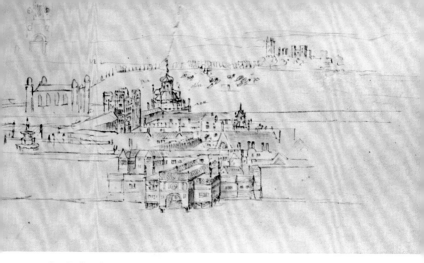

41. Whitehall Palace. York Place, the traditional Westminster residence of the Archbishops of York, was extensively rebuilt by Wolsey. Henry VIII remodeled it still further when it came into his hands after Wolsey's fall, and it was thereafter a principal royal residence until it was mostly destroyed by fires in the 1690s.

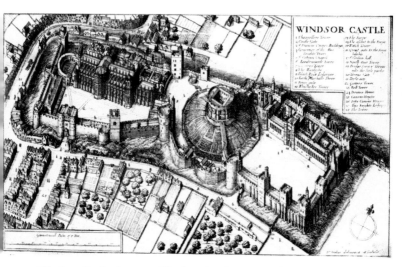

42. Windsor Castle. It was at Windsor Castle, on 11 July 1531, that Henry saw Catherine of Aragon for the last time.

Opposite: 40. Archbishop Warham, by Holbein. It is easy to believe Catherine of Aragon's claim that this lugubrious clergyman's mantra was 'the wrath of the prince is death'. Warham's death in 1532 opened the way to the appointment of Thomas Cranmer as his successor, and thus to the annulment of Henry's first marriage.

HENRICVS. viii.

ANA BOLLINA · VXOR HEN VIII

45. Design for a pageant tableau, by Holbein. This tableau of Apollo and the
Muses was designed by Holbein for the German merchants of the 'Steelyard'
(the Hanseatic League's London trading station), who staged it as their
contribution to the pageant in honour of Anne Boleyn on 31 May 1533, the
eve of her coronation.

Previous pages: 43. & 44. Later 'long gallery' copies of portraits of Henry and
Anne Boleyn. The Henry here is clearly derived from the Holbein sketch, but
no original survives for this well-known representation of Anne.

46. Calais, from a sixteenth-century chart. Henry and Anne crossed to Calais together in October 1532, for a summit conference with Francis I in Boulogne, at which he promised diplomatic support to Henry in his campaign for a divorce.

47. A lady in waiting at Henry's Court, by Holbein. If the label 'M Souch' is correct, then this young woman would be either Mrs Anne Zouche, a lady in waiting to Anne Boleyn, or Mary Zouch, a lady in waiting to Jane Seymour. Either way it gives us a good picture of a lady about Court in the 1530s.

Anglici Matrimonij

Sententia diffinitiua

Lata per sanctissimum. Dñm Nostrum. D. Clementem. Papã. vij. in sacro Consistorio de
Reuerendissimorum Dominorum. S. R. E. Cardinalium consilio super validitate Ma
trimonij inter Serenissimos Henricum. VIII. & Catherinam Angliæ Reges contracti.

PRO.

Eadem Serenissima Catherina Angliæ Regina,

CONTRA.

Serenissimum Henricum. VIII. Angliæ Regem.

Clemens Papa. vij.

Hristi nomine inuocato in Trono iustitiæ pro tribunali sedentes, & solum Deum præ oculis habentes, Per hanc
nostram diffinitiuam sententiam quam de Venerabilium Fratrum nostrorum Sanctæ Ro. Ec. Car. Consistorialiter
coram nobis congregatorum Consilio, & assensu ferimus in his scriptis, pronunciamus, decernimus, & declaramus,
in causa, & causis ad nos, & Sedem Apostolicam per appellationem, per charissimam in christo filiam Ca
therinam Angliæ Reginam Illustrem a nostris, & Sedis Apostolicæ Legatis in Regno Angliæ deputatis interposi
tam legitime deuolutis, & aduocatis, inter prædictam Catherinam Reginam, & Charissimum in christo filium Henricum. VIII.
Angliæ Regem Illustrem, super Validitate, & inualiditate matrimonij inter eosdem Reges contracti, & consumati rebusφ alijs in
actis, causæ & causarum huiusmodi latius deductis, & dilecto filio Paulo Capissucho causarum sacri palatij tunc decano & pro
pter ipsius Pauli absentiam Venerabili Fratri nostro Iacobo Simonetæ Episcopo Pisauriēn. vnius ex dictis palatij causarum Audito
ribus locumtenens, audiendis instruendis, & in Consistorio nostro Secreto referendis commissis, & per eos nobis, & eisdem Car
dinalibus Relatis, & mature discussis, coram nobis pendentibus, Matrimonium inter prædictos Catherinam, & Henricum An
gliæ Reges contractum, & inde secuta quæcunφ fuisse, & esse validum, & canonicum validaφ, & Canonica, suoφ debitos de
buisse, & debere sortiri effectus, prolemφ exinde susceptam, & suscipiendam fuisse, & fore legitimam, & præfatum Henri
cum Angliæ Regem teneri, & obligatum fuisse, et fore ad cohabitandum cum dicta Catherina Regina eius legitima coniuge, illamφ
maritali affectione, & Regio honore tractandum, & eundem Henricum Angliæ Regem ad præmissa omnia, & singula cum
effectu adimplendum condemnandum omnibusφ iuris Remedijs cogendum, & compellendum fore, prout condemnamus, cogimus, &
compellimus, Molestationesφ, & denegationes Per eundem Henricum Regem eidem Catherinæ Reginæ super inualiditate, ac fœ
dere dictis Matrimonij quomodolibet factas, & præstitas fuisse, & esse illicitas, & iniustas, & eidem Henrico Regi super il
lis ac inualiditate matrimonij huiusmodi perpetuam Silentium imponendum fore, & imponimus, eiusdemφ Henricum Angliæ Re
gem in expensis in huiusmodi causa pro parte dictæ Catherinæ Reginæ coram nobis, & dictis omnibus legitime factis condem
nandum fore, & condemnamus, quarum expensarum taxationem nobis imposterum reseruamus.

Ita pronunciauimus .J.

Lata fuit Romæ in Palatio Apostolico publice in Consistorio die. XXIII. Martij. M. D. XXXIIII.

Blosius.

48. Clement VII's judgment against Henry. After calling in vain upon the
king to leave Anne and take back his first wife, Clement VII finally issued his
'definitive sentence' in favour of Catherine of Aragon on 23 March 1534.

Opposite: 49. Thomas More, by Holbein. Thomas More's execution on
6 July 1535 was the culmination of a series of public executions designed
to strike fear into the hearts of those who might consider denying
Henry's claim to be Supreme Head of the Church of England.

51. Sir Richard Southwell, by Holbein. Sir Richard Southwell was an East Anglian gentleman who did particularly well out of the English Reformation, owing his advancement to the patronage of both the Duke of Norfolk and Thomas Cromwell. He was present at the conversation in the Tower of London during which, according to the testimony of Richard Rich, Thomas More actually denied Henry's supreme headship. However, questioned in court, Southwell said he had heard nothing. This is Holbein's sketch for what was a particularly fine portrait.

50. Sir John Godsalve, by Holbein. Another big winner of the 1530s was John Godsalve, Clerk of the Signet and, like Southwell, a client and supporter of Cromwell's.

Opposite: 52. Derived from the Holbein image, this is a later portrayal of Jane Seymour for the 'long gallery' market. Jane's success in bearing Henry a son made her his favourite wife, and they are buried together at Windsor.

53. Jane Seymour's badge. Jane Seymour's phoenix badge beneath the imperial crown and above the Tudor rose, in stained glass once in the Seymour residence of Wolf Hall. The glass is now in the nearby church of Great Bedwyn.

54. Edward VI. Despite the sad death after childbirth of Jane, Henry was carried away with joy at the birth of Edward, his longed-for son and heir.

55. The barn at Wolf Hall. Wolf Hall, the seat of Sir John Seymour, was probably the birthplace of Jane Seymour. The house itself was long ago demolished, but this barn survived until it burned down in the early twentieth century. According to local legend, Henry and Jane were married in this barn, but in fact they were married at York Place (Whitehall) on 30 May 1536.

57. Henry VIII. This miniature portrait is from the 'Bosworth Jewel', a set of miniatures produced by Nicholas Hilliard to illustrate the Tudor succession.

58. Henry VIII. A sketch of Henry VIII by Thomas Smith (1513-77), in the margin of one of his books. Reproduced by kind permission of the President and Fellows of Queens' College, Cambridge.

59. Tomb of Henry Fitzroy. Henry Fitzroy, the king's illegitimate son by Elizabeth Blount, was perhaps being considered for a place in the succession in the 1520s, but was well out of the running by the time he died in 1536. His burial was arranged by the Duke of Norfolk, his father-in-law, and he was originally laid to rest in Thetford Priory church, in effect a mausoleum of the ducal family. At the dissolution of the monasteries his remains were transferred to the church at Framlingham, which was also under ducal patronage, and where this fine tomb was later erected by the family in his memory.

Previous page: 56. Henry VIII and Henry VII, by Holbein. This cartoon was part of Holbein's design for a mural at Whitehall showing Henry, his father, his mother, and Jane Seymour. Here we first see Holbein's iconic image of Henry, curiously reminiscent of the pose he gave to Thomas More's fool, Henry Patenson, in the group portrait of ten years before. Holbein's mural was probably the first full-length, life-size and lifelike portrait of an English king.

Right: 60. Thomas Boleyn, Earl of Wiltshire. Despite the executions of his son George and his daughter Anne in 1536, Thomas Boleyn himself died in his bed at Hever Castle in 1538. His funeral brass in St Peter's Church there, the only known likeness, shows him in the regalia of a Knight of the Garter.

Below: 61. Declaration by the bishops. This declaration, probably from 1536, explains that two disputed scriptural texts (John 20:21 and Acts 20:28) confer spiritual, but not political, power upon bishops, and then goes on to explain that scripture testifies to the 'highnesse and excellencye' of Christian princes, who have the power if 'busshopes be negligent ... to se theym doo ther dutie'.

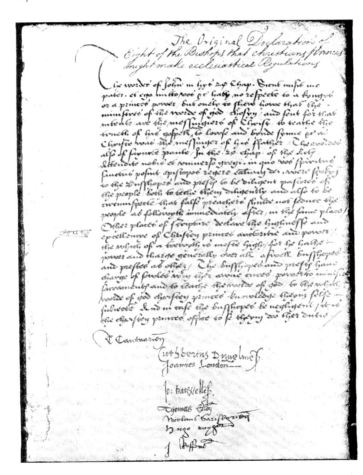

63. Detail from the title-page to the Hagiographa in the Great Bible (1539). Henry VIII hands copies of the Bible to Cranmer on his right and to Cromwell on his left. Thomas Cranmer stands bare-headed in the presence of his king, his mitre at his feet. This beautifully and expensively coloured copy is from the library of St John's College, Cambridge, where a college tradition says that it originally belonged to Thomas Cromwell himself. Reproduced by kind permission of the Master and Fellows of St John's College, Cambridge.

Opposite: 62. Mary ('Madge') Shelton, by Holbein. If the label is correct, then this is Mary Shelton, later Lady Heveningham, thought to have been one of Henry's later mistresses.

¶ The Byble in
Englyfhe, that is to faye the con-
tent of all the holy fcrypture, bothe
of ÿ olde and newe teftament, truly
translated after the veryte of the
hebrue and Greke textes, by ÿ dy-
lygent studye of dyuerse excellent
learned men, expert in the forfayde
tonges.

¶ Prynted by Rychard Grafton ₮
Edward Whitchurch.

Cum priuilegio ad imprimen-
dum folum.
1539.

65. Act of Six Articles. This excerpt from the Statute Roll gives the six articles of faith and practice that Henry imposed on his Church of England by statute in 1539, starting with the affirmation of the traditional doctrine of the real presence, and ending with the enforcement of the practice of confession.

Opposite: 64. Title-page of the Great Bible, 1539. Enthroned as God's vicar, Henry symbolically hands out the Word of God to the spiritual and temporal hierarchies of his realm, headed respectively by Cranmer on his right and by Cromwell on his left. The preacher (bottom left) proclaims what was for Henry the Bible's chief message: 'Obey the prince...', and his grateful subjects, duly enlightened, chorus 'Long live the king'.

66. Henry VIII as David. This is the first of several pictures which illustrate a stunningly beautiful manuscript book of the Psalms that was produced for Henry's personal use in 1540. Pictures in books of the Psalms often showed the biblical King David, believed to have been their author. In this copy, David is shown with the features of Henry himself.

67. Anne of Cleves, by Barthel Bruyn.

68. Anne of Cleves House. Now a museum, this house in Lewes formed part of the settlement with which Henry compensated Anne of Cleves for abruptly ending their marriage.

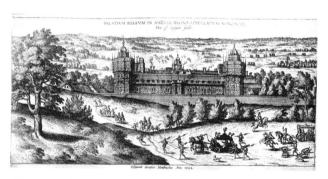

Above: 69. Nonsuch. Henry VIII's fantasy palace was built around 1541 out of materials recycled from suppressed monasteries. One of Elizabeth's favourite residences, it fell into disuse and disrepair under the Stuarts, and Charles II used it to pay off one of his discarded mistresses, Barbara Villiers, who demolished it and sold it off for scrap in 1682.

71. Hever Castle, once the seat of the Boleyn family, was also made over to Anne of Cleves as part of her settlement.

Opposite below right: 70. Mary Queen of Scots. This Elizabethan miniature shows Mary Queen of Scots, who as a young child was betrothed to Prince Edward by the Treaty of Greenwich (1543).

Above: 72. Oatlands (Surrey), one of Henry's many palaces, where he married Catherine Howard on 28 July 1540.

73. The Act of Succession, 1544. This section of the act spells out the oath that must be taken by all clergymen and royal officials, renouncing the 'Bisshopp of Rome' (the Pope) and promising to uphold the statute's determination of the order of the succession.

74. The Family of Henry VIII, ca. 1545.
There is a clear dynastic message in this
group image from Henry's declining years.
Jane Seymour and his son Edward, first
in the succession, flank the king, while his
daughters, both then classified as illegitimate,
literally wait in the wings, in case the
legitimate line expires.

75. Design for a timepiece, by Holbein.
Holbein's sketch for a timepiece, designed
and built by Nicholas Kratzer, that was made
for Sir Anthony Denny, who presented to
the king as a New Year's gift at the start of
1545.

76. & 77. Even Henry VIII's will (30 December 1546) was signed with 'dry stamp'. This section bequeaths his 'imperial crown' to Mary (pictured opposite) in the event of Edward's death without issue. Note that while Edward is described as Henry's 'deeerest sonne prince Edward', Mary is simply his 'daughter'.

78. Henry VIII's signature, which in his last years was embossed into documents with the 'dry stamp' and inked in to save him the labour of writing.

79. Elizabeth. The 'Lady Elizabeth' of Henry VIII's later years, illegitimate but acknowledged as third in line for the throne, is shown here in a simple but fine portrait that emphasises status through its expensive colour and her fine dress, and piety in the books open and held.

MARIA : REGINA.

80. St George's Chapel, Windsor. Henry VIII chose St George's Windsor, rather than his father's Lady Chapel in Westminster Abbey, as his final resting place, and he lies there alongside Jane Seymour.

81. Thomas Howard, 3rd Duke of Norfolk. This copy of the Holbein portrait of Thomas Howard, 3rd Duke of Norfolk, shows him in ducal ermine with the collar of the Garter, and with the Earl Marshal's baton in his right hand and the Lord Treasurer's staff in his left. The sudden fall from favour of the duke and his son in late 1546 was one of the turning-points of Tudor history.

irreversibly committed to the revolutionary policies of the 1530s, and the only way to reverse them was to remove him from the throne. This solution was simply beyond the mental horizon of the Pilgrims.

Henry reluctantly accepted Norfolk's *fait accompli* and, having done so, threw himself into the play with something approaching enthusiasm. Robert Aske was invited to Court for Christmas, where he was entertained and rewarded royally, and was reassured to hear from the king's own lips reiterated promises of a Parliament at York, the defence of the faith against innovators, and the redress of northern grievances. But when an unstable northern knight, Sir Francis Bigod (ironically, one of the few northerners sympathetic to religious change and really enthusiastic for the royal supremacy), attempted for reasons of his own to raise the standard of rebellion anew early in 1537, Henry was quick to seize the chance for revenge. The embers of revolt were stamped out, in fact, by many of the local gentry who had themselves risen the previous autumn. But Henry reckoned this betrayal released him from the promises Norfolk had made in his name. He ordered exemplary executions across the north, and had the ringleaders of the original Pilgrimage brought to London for trial and execution. It was not justice, but it was a brutal display of power. Henry would see no further rebellions in England.

The politics of 1536 were certainly the most complex of any year of Henry's reign, and the year itself has as good a claim as any to be considered 'the' crucial year of the reign – more because of what did not happen than because of what did. Most importantly, it did not see Anne Boleyn bear a son, a failure which played a large part in her downfall. Her fall, in turn, might have meant the end for the men who had done so much to put her on the throne, Cromwell and Cranmer – but they survived and even came out of the debacle ahead. With Catherine of Aragon and Anne Boleyn both dead, many conservatives, such as Stephen Gardiner in his virtual exile at the French court, hoped for a rapprochement with Rome. Their hopes were in vain. Cranmer and Cromwell, having survived, might in their turn have hoped for a more decisive lurch towards the religious policies of the Reformation, but Henry himself drew back and curbed them. Finally, the great rebellion of autumn 1536, the Pilgrimage of Grace, might have reversed his policy by main force: indeed, might have cost him his throne. It did neither, and Henry emerged stronger than ever. 1536 was one of the most indecisively decisive years in English history. What it showed about Henry was his reluctance to go back.

10

REFORMATION &
REACTION:
1537 - 1539

Instead of reversing Henry's policies, the Pilgrims had if anything only managed to entrench them. There was no way Henry could even consider going back without looking as though he was bowing to pressure. Cromwell and Cranmer therefore managed to advance the cause of religious change. Smaller monasteries continued to be closed down, and royal fury at monastic involvement in the Pilgrimage accelerated the process. Some were taken into the king's hands by forfeiture on the grounds that their abbots had been guilty of treason. Others voluntarily surrendered into the king's hands for fear of the same charge. Henry had been infuriated by the involvement of monks and friars in the Pilgrimage, and from this time showed no love for the 'religious life'. 1537 saw the compilation of a new, full statement of the doctrine of the Church of England, the product of lengthy and often fraught discussions between representatives of the conservative and the evangelical factions among the higher clergy, led respectively by John Stokesley (Bishop of London) and Cranmer. Under normal circumstances, this was the sort of project into which Henry would have thrown himself with enthusiasm. However, he had more pressing concerns even than religion. His new queen was expecting their first child, and Henry was too excited to worry about catechisms. Jane bore him a son on 12 October, and the new book, the *Institution of a Christian Man*, was handed to him for approval around the same time. Preoccupied with the delights of fatherhood, he simply nodded it through. However, rather than issue it in his own name, he had it set forth in the name of the bishops (it was commonly known as the Bishops' Book), and only for a trial period of three years. When, later, he found time to examine the book in detail, he found much to cavil at.

The christening of Edward on 15 October – the last christening of an English prince to be conducted amid the full ceremonies of the Catholic liturgy – was one of the high moments of Henry's life. God seemed to be smiling on him, and not even the tragic death of Jane Seymour from complications following a difficult birth could cast a shadow over his joy. Reconciliation within the royal family was symbolised by the role of his elder daughter, Mary, as Edward's godmother. Archbishop Cranmer was one godfather, and the Dukes of Norfolk and Suffolk also enjoyed this distinction. Soon afterwards, Norfolk was entrusted with the less happy task of commissioning Masses and prayers for Queen Jane's soul.

Cromwell and Cranmer continued to press on with religious change, and in 1538 Henry was persuaded to go a little further down the road of replacing the saint-based piety of late medieval Christianity with the Bible-based religion of Protestantism. Customs such as going on pilgrimage to shrines which held the wonder-working relics or images of saints, or of lighting votive candles before images, were abruptly redefined as idolatry. This was a particularly dramatic change for a king who on these matters, in the view of one Protestant contemporary, 'till God opened his eyes, was as blind and obstinate as the rest'. This radical shift was facilitated by the fact that the Bishops' Book had re-edited and re-numbered the traditional Ten Commandments to bring them into line with the version favoured by some Protestant reformers and thus to give more prominence to the divine prohibition against the making and worshipping of 'graven images'. To drive the point home, the great shrines of England were closed down in a nationwide campaign that summer. The relic of Christ's blood at Hailes in Gloucestershire was brought to London and publicly burned, as was the great statue of Our Lady which had been venerated for centuries at Walsingham in Norfolk.

The campaign culminated at the end of September with the destruction of perhaps England's most famous shrine, that of St Thomas at Canterbury. It had been a hard job to convince Henry VIII to sanction the iconoclasm of 1538. Hugh Latimer later commented on how difficult it had been to persuade the king to take down the Holy Blood of Hailes. But the destruction of the shrine of St Thomas showed that the king had identified himself wholeheartedly with the iconoclastic policy. Henry came to preside in person at the ceremonies on 8 September, which included the burning of Thomas's bones and the staging of a play by John Bale, a former friar turned zealous reformer, which turned on its head the traditional tale of Thomas's death. The burning was followed up by a proclamation which denied

St Thomas's claims to sanctity and martyrdom, denounced him as a traitor, and decreed that his feast days (there were three) were to be deleted from the calendar of the Church of England. Henceforth, St Thomas of Canterbury, martyr, was to be known as Thomas Becket, traitor.

Henry's growing disenchantment with the religious orders was symbolised by the burning of Friar John Forest. Forest was an Observant Franciscan, a member of the order which had resisted Henry in the early 1530s more steadfastly than any other group, and he had for a while served as confessor to Catherine of Aragon. Now he was condemned for both treason and heresy (he was the only Roman Catholic ever to be formally condemned for heresy by the Church of England) and was executed in a spectacularly gruesome fashion, hanging in chains over a pyre fuelled by a sacred wooden image fetched all the way from Wales. The combination of hanging and burning, first designed for Lollard rebels in the reign of Henry V, drew attention to the dual character of his offence.

Other public gestures that year demonstrated Henry's new-found hatred for monasticism. The bishop of London was charged in the King's Bench with the offence of 'praemunire' (a variety of treason, essentially that of seeking to implement a foreign jurisdiction within the king's domains) on the grounds that he had conducted the liturgical ceremony at which a monk made his final vows. The bishop was let off with a token fine, but the point was clear: no more monks and nuns were to be recruited in England. The 'voluntary' surrender of religious houses seen in the wake of the Pilgrimage of Grace was extended to monasteries which had not in any way offended against the law, and Henry's own two recent foundations, at Bisham and Stixwold, both surrendered into the king's hands. As if to confirm that he had in fact decided to close down all religious houses, in spring 1538 Henry issued a public denial of the widespread rumours to that effect. The process of suppression would not be complete until 1540, but its progress was inexorable.

A particularly important moment in the dissolution of the monasteries came with the extension of the policy towards the houses of friars late in 1538. The Observant Franciscans had already been closed down, but there were over two hundred other houses of Franciscans, Dominicans, Carmelites, and Austin friars across the land. While the monasteries (and to a lesser extent the nunneries) offered a really tempting financial prospect, the move against the friars shows that political and ideological considerations were now also at work. For the friars lacked the ample estates that often supported monasteries, and depended heavily on legacies, donations, Mass stipends, and on modest endowments made to support Masses for the dead. The inventories of their goods show that many offered very slim pickings. Apart from the sale of the usually urban plots on which the friaries stood, the best returns often came from the lead off the roofs as the buildings were torn down.

What mattered about the friars was first that they were still among the main providers of educated preaching, and second that to a much greater extent than the monks they formed part of international religious orders. Potentially they might in time have posed a threat to the new regime, fertile ground for a Counter-Reformation. In Catholic countries popular rebellions were often sparked off or sustained by the preaching of friars. The Prior of the Dominicans of York, Dr John Pickering, for example, had composed a poem that became in effect the marching song of the Pilgrims in autumn 1536. He had, of course, been executed. But the closure of the houses of friars was a kind of insurance policy against a recurrence of that threat. This can be seen in the documents with which the friars were often asked to surrender their houses, for many of them were required not simply to surrender their property to the king but to renounce and denounce their former way of life as superstitious and hypocritical.

The high tide of evangelical influence in Henry's Church of England was reached with the publication under royal patronage of the English Bible. Despite the traditional association of vernacular scripture with Lollardy, and its recent association with Lutheranism, Henry had always had some sympathy for it in principle. He had said as much in the early 1520s, in the open letter in which he urged the Dukes of Saxony to silence Luther. It was, after all, an idea which had been made fashionable by Erasmus before Luther appeared on the public stage. However, Henry and his bishops had laboured to suppress Tyndale's translation of the New Testament in the later 1520s, and it was only after the break with Rome, when so many conventional ecclesiastical attitudes were called into question, that the English Bible became practical politics. Both Cromwell and Cranmer were strongly in favour. Henry himself seems to have been convinced partly by the logic of the royal supremacy and partly by its rhetoric. Logically, in breaking with Rome, the Bible was the only alternative source of Christian authority to which appeal could credibly be made. This made the case for vernacular scripture difficult to resist. And in practice Henry VIII's preachers and propagandists appealed endlessly to the Bible, especially the Old Testament, to establish the authority of kings in general, and their authority over priests in particular. The 'Word of God' was invoked against the 'human traditions' of the Bishop of Rome. Indeed, it was in the 1530s that the description of the Bible as the 'Word of God' became current in English, largely because of its adoption in royal propaganda. The Word of God was regarded as a lesson in obedience, Henry's favourite virtue (in others). As John Bale put it in *King John*, a play celebrating Henry's triumph over the clergy:

> If Your Grace would cause God's Word to be taught sincerely,
> And subdue those priests that will not preach it truly,
> The people should know to their prince their lawful duty.

Parish churches were instructed to obtain English Bibles in the injunctions of 1536 and again in those of 1538. But although copies had been printed abroad in 1535 and 1537, it was not until 1539 that they became easily available. For that year saw the appearance of the 'Great Bible', financed by Cromwell, edited by Miles Coverdale, and published by Richard Grafton and Edward Whitchurch. Several editions followed over the next few years, with a lengthy preface by Cranmer added in 1540. Royal approval for the 'Great Bible' was vividly symbolised by the frontispiece (not in fact the work of Hans Holbein, though it is often said to be), which showed Henry VIII handing out the 'Word of God' to Cromwell and Cranmer for distribution to his grateful priests and people.

Even as the tide of religious change reached its height, circumstances were shifting at home and abroad. At home, the relaxation of pressure against heresy in the

1530s had fostered the emergence of one heresy Henry could not abide: 'sacramentarianism', denial of the real presence of Christ in the sacrament of the eucharist. Abroad, the destruction of the shrine of St Thomas had shocked Catholic Europe, and an outbreak of peace between France and Spain gave the Pope the chance to excommunicate Henry anew, with fair hope of seeing the sentence executed by the newly reconciled continental powers. Henry's response was twofold. First, he invested heavily in defence, especially coastal forts, many of which were built or rebuilt out of materials recycled from suppressed monasteries. Men were mustered for possible military service throughout the land. In summer 1539, Henry lorded it over a magnificent march-past of the mustered men of London, equipped in new uniforms of fine white cloth (at their own expense! – those who could not afford the uniform were not allowed to take part).

In addition, the king put the brake on religious change, most notably by presiding, in another dramatic personal intervention, at the show trial of a sacramentarian heretic, John Lambert, on 16 November 1538. Vested symbolically in white, Henry presided while his bishops disputed with Lambert in an effort to change his mind. Finally, Henry himself argued with him and urged him to recant, all to no avail. He personally instructed Cromwell to pronounce sentence upon Lambert, and that same day he issued a proclamation upholding traditional doctrines of the eucharist and of baptism against recent innovations. Even his more reformist bishops loathed the 'Anabaptists' (upholders of adult rather than infant baptism). But it was Henry himself who added the word 'sacramentaries' to the draft proclamation, thus potentially sweeping in many of the reformist bishops' friends. Some Dutch Anabaptists were burned a week after Lambert, to show that the proclamation meant business.

Among the bishops who assisted at Lambert's trial were two whose stars had been waning since the break with Rome, but who were now returning to favour. Stephen Gardiner had, at long last, been recalled from his three-year mission to France, and the bishop of Durham, Cuthbert Tunstall, also made himself useful as the king cast around for willing helpers in the suppression of heresy. Gardiner and Tunstall appealed to the more conservative side of the king's character, and were prominent in manoeuvres which led, in spring 1539, to the passage of the Act of Six Articles against sacramentarianism and one or two other religious bugbears of the king's, notably the marriage of priests. Henry's hand can be seen in the draconian sweep of this act, which enjoined burning as the penalty for a first offence (traditional heresy law in England had allowed for escape by recantation for first offenders). Under these fierce new powers, a vigorous campaign against heresy was launched in London in the king's name. At the same time, Henry made a show of observing traditional Church ceremonies in 1539, making sure that foreign ambassadors came along to see. They duly reported home that Henry was Catholic about everything except the Pope and the plunder of the clergy. As most kings might find themselves in conflict with the Pope from time to time, and were often obliged to tap the wealth of the Church, Henry now seemed much less alien than before.

While the Pope was proceeding against Henry VIII on account of his pillaging of shrines and monasteries, Henry initiated proceedings of his own against the

English relatives of Cardinal Reginald Pole, who was entrusted with the task of implementing papal sanctions against the king. Evidence against those involved in the so-called 'Exeter conspiracy' was elicited from Sir Geoffrey Pole, the rather suggestible younger brother of the cardinal, in exchange for his life. The victims executed in December included the Marquis of Exeter (Pole's cousin), Henry, Lord Montague (Pole's brother) and Sir Edward Neville (brother to Lord Abergavenny and a prominent courtier). They were belatedly followed in February 1539 by Sir Nicholas Carew, the Master of the King's Horse. Terror rather than justice was the object. Unable to get at Cardinal Pole, Henry had to make do with destroying his family – and thus thinning the ranks of possible non-Tudor claimants to the throne. The element of sheer vengeance in all this is seen in the treatment of the cardinal's mother, the aged Margaret, Countess of Salisbury (a niece of Edward IV). Condemned in 1539 in an act of attainder which wrapped up condemnations of a host of Henry's enemies (both living and dead) she was kept in the Tower until 1541, when she was executed on 27 May. Executions such as these made it clear that no one, however nobly born, was above the law, and no one, however powerful, was secure from the wrath of the prince. No English king ever shed more noble blood than Henry VIII. Where his father had taken their money, Henry took their lives, and often on equally flimsy pretexts. As much as his father, he deserved the fully-fledged baronial revolt that he never faced. The fact that neither of them faced it is an index of how English politics was changing.

11

THE FALL OF CROMWELL: 1540

The increasing influence of conservative churchmen around Henry was an implicit threat to the dominance of Thomas Cromwell, who strove to counter it by pursuing his own favourite policy: alliance with the Protestant princes of Germany. A somewhat flattering portrait by Hans Holbein helped him convince Henry to take a new bride from one of those princely dynasties, that of the Duke of Cleves. The marriage which might have saved Cromwell's career actually ended it. Although Henry's marriage to Anne of Cleves was celebrated on 6 January 1540, it was never consummated. Henry found his new wife unattractive, and the embarrassment of impotence in her company led him to reject with equal ferocity the marriage and its architect. Worked on by the Duke of Norfolk and Bishop Stephen Gardiner, who at some point waved before his eyes the shapely person of the duke's teenage niece, Catherine Howard, Henry set in motion the well-worn wheels of divorce. Anne of Cleves was more flexible than Catherine of

Aragon, and accepted a reasonable financial settlement with something like good grace. She spent the rest of her life in relative comfort in England.

Cromwell was not so lucky. Vengeful as ever, Henry turned the full force of his wrath upon him. As recently as April 1540 Cromwell had been rewarded with elevation to the earldom of Essex, but the decade of revolution in Henry's reign was brought to a close with the new earl's dramatic arrest in the Council Chamber on 10 June 1540. The pace of religious change had already slowed almost to a halt, and the debacle of the Cleves marriage temporarily reduced Cromwell's credibility to zero. That window of opportunity was all his enemies needed to persuade the king that he had been fomenting heresy and meditating treason. The latter charge was of course absurd, but there was enough substance in the former, and the reliable Richard Rich was as willing as ever to see to the legal niceties. Cromwell was convicted by attainder without trial – a crime which was ironically suited to the punishment he had so often meted out to others – and he went to his death on 28 July 1540 protesting his loyalty and his orthodoxy (although his confession of belief in fact included nothing which a convinced Lutheran could not have said in perfect good faith).

The fall of Cromwell precipitated one of the defining achievements of the reign of Henry VIII, the formal establishment of the Privy Council as a department of government. Although in some ways a traditional institution (kings had always had their councils), and although in others a creation of Thomas Cromwell's (the name 'Privy Council' first appears in the 1530s, notably when Henry VIII was refuting the Pilgrims' charge that he was surrounded with baseborn, evil councillors), the Privy Council only came into its own with Cromwell's fall. Henry never again allowed one man to dominate policy as Wolsey and Cromwell had done in their day. The Privy Council was to become the primary instrument for the formulation and execution of the sovereign's will for the next century or so. In the immediate term, its significance perhaps lay more in the new rules of courtly precedence which were associated with it. Although men of noble birth were frequently recruited to the council and held high office under the Crown, and although gentlemen who worked their way up to the council in royal service were often rewarded with peerages, Henry VIII laid down rules by which the highest officers of royal government and household as such took precedence over nobles, whatever their rank. This was in effect to underline the point he had made to the Pilgrims in 1536, that nobility derived from and depended upon the Crown, and that its ultimate criterion was not so much birth as service to the king.

On 8 August 1540, less than a fortnight after Cromwell's execution, Henry VIII married Catherine Howard. Unfortunately for Norfolk and Gardiner, the weapon which they had deployed against Cromwell was, though powerful, unstable, and in the end blew up in their faces. Catherine may have inflamed the passion of the middle-aged king, but his feelings were not entirely reciprocated. During their summer progress in 1541, which for the first and only time in the reign took the royal household to the north (reaching York by way of Lincoln, Gainsborough and Pontefract), she began to hanker for the company of one of her old friends and suitors, Thomas Culpeper, a Gentleman of the Privy Chamber. Their nocturnal assignations were relatively discreet, and although it would only have been a matter of time, they had not in fact become lovers when the court returned to the south in autumn. They were not to get the chance. It was shortly after Henry VIII's return to Hampton Court that Archbishop Cranmer shared with his sovereign, by means of a tactful letter, some extremely disturbing news, namely, that Catherine had enjoyed intimate sexual relationships with two young men before her marriage to Henry. Her frank confession of the youthful indiscretions which a delicate but thorough investigation soon brought to light might just have saved her. But once the hounds caught the scent of her summer dalliance with Culpeper, her fate was sealed. They had not become lovers, but her record made it impossible to credit the innocence of their intentions (which they made no attempt to maintain). Catherine was condemned for treason by act of attainder, and was beheaded on 13 February 1542. The act included a declaration that it was treason for a woman to marry the king if she had had premarital sex. As the Imperial ambassador caustically observed, this rather narrowed the field.

It was a year and a half later, on 12 June 1543, that Henry took his sixth and last wife, Catherine Parr, a mature but still relatively young widow (it was premarital sex, not previous marriage, that constituted treason), the sister of one of his Privy Councillors, William Parr. But by this stage sex may not have been a priority for the aging and ailing king. As late as 1540, in the aftermath of his disastrous wedding night with Anne of Cleves, Henry had anxiously reassured his closest advisers of his continuing virility. It was Anne's unattractiveness, he insisted, that prevented him from consummating the marriage. But this looks like bravado. Neither of his last two wives was so much as thought to have become pregnant by him. Catherine Howard had clearly begun to look elsewhere. And while Catherine Parr was impeccably faithful to Henry, she remarried with almost indecent haste after his death. Her new husband (her third), was Thomas Seymour, one of the uncles of Edward VI, and she was pregnant within months. Henry's health was generally worsening throughout the 1540s. He was persistently troubled by a festering sore in his leg, and was massively overweight. It was in this context that, in 1544, Henry put through his final Act of Succession, which established the succession, in order, on Edward, Mary and Elizabeth, tacitly passed over the Scottish line of the Stuarts, descended from his elder sister, Margaret, and provided that, in the event of his own line failing, the succession should pass to the heirs of his younger sister, Mary, who had married the Duke of Suffolk.

12

THE LATTER YEARS: 1541 - 1545

To speak of a foreign policy holiday through the 1530s would be an exaggeration, as English ambassadors criss-crossed Europe seeking alliances, trying to forestall papal countermeasures, and spreading Henry's new gospel of royal supremacy. But Henry's policies had put him into virtual isolation, and for years he was all but irrelevant to the rivalry between the Habsburg and Valois monarchies, which was the central axis of European affairs. In 1538, when he ceased to be an irrelevance, it was only so as to become a potential target. But some well-timed displays of religious conservatism had helped avert that danger. Now, in the 1540s, his dynastic problems had been resolved, and the pace of religious change had been slowed almost to a standstill. In addition, the consequent tensions in English politics had been relaxed thanks to the destruction of Cromwell, and the plunder of the Church had made him richer than any previous English king. Henry was once more in a position to contemplate a return to his overriding political ambition: that of conquest in France. The monarchy was very different after the turmoil of the 1530s. But the monarch was very much the same, even if he had added some new ideas to the old ones.

The military campaigns of the 1540s were in some ways a replay of those of the 1510s. However, this time Henry decided to deal with the threat of Scottish intervention by a pre-emptive strike. Diplomatic pressure and border incidents of increasing ferocity culminated in English military action which was as politically decisive in the long term as it was tactically futile at the time. The Duke of Norfolk was entrusted with the task of chastising the Scots in October 1542, but his raid was a fiasco, and probably cost the raiders more than their victims. Norfolk's stock sank: the hero of 1536 now looked something of a clown, and Henry would turn elsewhere for military leadership in future. However, the Scottish riposte was the customary catastrophe. A huge force of Scots underwent a crushing defeat at Solway Moss (November 1542). Where James IV had died in battle, James V died from the shock on hearing of the scale of the defeat.

Now, inspired by the imperial rhetoric of the royal supremacy and by the knowledge of traditional English claims to sovereignty over Scotland which had been unearthed in the course of researching that supremacy, Henry went fully onto the political rather than the military offensive in Scotland. In the power vacuum left by the death of James V he succeeded in putting together an Anglophile lobby among the Scottish aristocracy, using a judicious combination of religious propaganda and financial inducements. Scotland, like England, was feeling the first stirrings of Protestantism, and those with evangelical sympathies saw better prospects for change through alignment with Henry VIII's rejection of Rome. At the same time, disaffected Scottish nobles saw their best chance of displacing the hitherto dominant figure of Cardinal Beaton – a sort of Scottish Wolsey, a little slimmer and a lot poorer – through moving in the direction at least of Henry's Reformation. Negotiations with this new grouping in Scottish politics led to the Treaty of Greenwich (1 July 1543), in which it was agreed that the new Queen of Scots, the infant Mary, would marry the young Prince Edward, thus uniting the crowns in perpetuity. But the kaleidoscopic rotations of Scottish politics soon saw the treaty repudiated when the rival faction, Catholic and Francophile, regained control. So, while Henry prepared for war with France, a second, punitive strike against Scotland was planned. It was not to Norfolk that Henry turned this time, however, but to Edward Seymour, Earl of Hertford and uncle to Prince Edward, whose honour had thus been injured. In May 1544 he attacked Edinburgh by land and sea, devastating the Lowlands. Returning laden with plunder, Seymour's stock rose as Norfolk's had fallen.

With the Scots knocked out of the war, Henry trained his sights on France. Several years of assiduous diplomacy had restored the traditional Anglo-Imperial axis, and in the previous year Henry had already provided troops to fight for Charles V in the Netherlands. Now, despite his declining health – the problems in his legs alone would have immobilised a lesser man – Henry VIII crossed the Channel for the fourth and last time in July 1544, once more bent on conquest. He was no longer in any condition to lead his men in battle, so he established a central command in Calais while two armies sallied forth against the French. The first, under the Duke of Norfolk, laid siege in vain to Montreuil. The second, under the

Duke of Suffolk, successfully laid siege to Boulogne, taking it in September. Norfolk's stock continued its fall. The campaign of 1544 expired when, as before in the 1510s, Henry was suddenly let down by his ally, who made a separate peace at Crépy just days after the fall of Boulogne. At least Henry came away with something.

A more welcome lesson learned in the 1540s was the absolute importance to English security of a strong navy. Henry himself was perhaps more interested in his ships as an offensive force, or at least as a display of might. But even if glory and display were his aims, Henry's concern with and expenditure on the navy were vindicated in 1545. Having made peace with Charles V, Francis I attempted to turn the tables on Henry by invading across the Channel. But his fleet was beaten back from the Isle of Wight in a naval action second only to the defeat of the Spanish Armada in the annals of Tudor seamanship, but now, somewhat unfairly, remembered chiefly for the foundering of the Mary Rose before she had even left the harbour approaches. (The over-gunning of the Mary Rose, which contributed to its foundering, is somehow typical of Henry, both in the boundless and groundless faith in his own ingenuity which caused him to interfere in the design and refitting of the ship, and in the naïve faith that more is always better which flawed the design itself.) This setback to the French was the first of many which would frustrate enemies over the next 400 years, as increasing naval strength rendered England increasingly secure from invasion. Politically and militarily, the campaigns of 1545 blooded the new generation of Tudor statesmen and commanders. Around 100,000 men were mobilised at home against the threat of invasion. John Russell (Lord Russell) commanded by land, and the rising star John Dudley (Lord Lisle) by sea. Seymour, at first entrusted with the defence of Boulogne, was later in 1545 once more unleashed against the Scots.

The fall of Cromwell was to some extent a result of the halting of religious changes in the later 1530s, and it seemed to open the way to a reversal of those changes. In the event, Henry was characteristically reluctant to retreat. The tone for the remainder of his reign was set by the black humour of 30 July 1540, two days after Cromwell's execution, when Henry sent six dissidents to their deaths. Three of them (Edward Powell, Thomas Abel and Richard Fetherston) were Catholic priests who had spent years in the Tower of London after supporting Catherine of Aragon and refusing the oaths of succession and supremacy. The other three were Protestant preachers (Robert Barnes, William Jerome and Thomas Garrett) who had enjoyed royal patronage in the 1530s and had been zealous in promoting the supremacy. None had been tried in a court of law: an act of attainder spared the expense of a trial. They were drawn to their deaths in pairs, a Catholic and a Protestant side by side on a hurdle, the Catholics to be hanged and butchered, the Protestants to be burned at the stake. The point was unmistakable. The fact that Henry was not prepared to tolerate heresy did not for one moment mean that he was going to compromise on the royal supremacy.

It was around this time that Henry turned his attention to the official doctrinal position of his Church, giving close personal scrutiny to the Bishops' Book which he had approved on a temporary basis in 1537. He was far from happy with the tone of much of it, and engaged in a vigorous debate with Cranmer and others about how it should be amended. In particular, Cranmer sought to persuade Henry to a form of words which would at least not exclude the key Protestant doctrine of justification. He hoped that Henry would accept a distinction between 'justification by faith alone' and 'justification by faith only'. Essentially, many evangelicals were prepared to abandon the formula 'justification by faith alone', which was so offensive to Catholic sensibilities, on the grounds that while true faith was never 'alone' (in that it was always accompanied by charity, the love of God and the love of neighbour), the justification of the sinner before God was nevertheless achieved 'only' by faith. But Henry did not fall for it. He argued the matter at length with his archbishop, who eventually confessed himself convinced – though it is difficult to believe that he spoke the truth, in that the Protestant doctrine was plainly set out in the homilies he authorised for the Church of England within months of Henry's death.

The task of producing the revised text was entrusted to a select committee of half a dozen bishops and theologians. Their revisions were almost all of a markedly conservative character, in accordance with the clear wishes of the king. On the key issue, their final text specifically excluded both 'faith alone' and 'faith only'. On other matters, they reiterated traditional teachings on the eucharist, and left rather more room than the Bishops' Book had done for the intercession of the saints and prayer for the dead. The outcome of their labours was published in 1543 as *A Necessary Doctrine and Erudition for any Christian Man* (and was given statutory backing by the Act for the Advancement of True Religion later that year). It was commonly known as the 'King's Book', because it was described on the title page as 'set forth by the king's majesty', and had a preface written by him. Henry was as happy as ever to play the theologian, preening himself on his efforts 'to purge and cleanse our realm' from 'hypocrisy and superstition', and magisterially reproving his subjects for their 'inclination to sinister understanding of scripture, presumption, arrogancy, carnal liberty and contention'.

Henry's ecclesiastical policy in the 1540s combined the repression of heresy, especially sacramentarian heresy, with some mild measures of reform and continued plunder of the Church. Having disposed of the monasteries, he turned his attention to the collegiate churches, first picking them off piecemeal by 'surrender' and later passing a statute (1545) permitting him to dissolve ecclesiastical institutions at will. In addition, he carried on cherry-picking houses and estates from his bishops by means of exchanges which were distinctly to his advantage. Thanks to methods such as these, by the end of the reign he had more houses than he knew what to do with. Such reform as transpired was mainly the work of his archbishop, Thomas Cranmer, who was continually proposing alterations designed to edge the Church of England a little closer towards the Protestantism of Europe without alarming Henry about heresy. Thus he was able to persuade Henry to sanction an English version of the Litany (prayers of general intercession) in 1544, and next year to follow this with a complete English prayer book, or 'primer', for private use. The way in which he sold this policy to the king can be seen from the prayer book's preface, written in Henry's name. Here, the king proclaimed his confidence that this new book would help his subjects learn their 'duties to God, their king, and their neighbour'. Placing himself between God and neighbour, he showed not only his sense of his own special place in the order of creation, but also his complacent assumption of the viability of his peculiar ecclesiastical compromise. If there was any kind of direction in the development of English religion in these years it was not so much towards Protestantism as, precisely, towards a more English religion.

The religious fissures which had opened among English élites during the 1530s assumed considerable importance in politics after Cromwell. Court faction, which at its extreme became a matter of life and death for the leading players, took religion as its badge. The combination of political rivalry with theological division was a powerful mixture under a suspicious yet pious king. In 1543 Bishop Gardiner sought to destroy his great rival, the evangelical Archbishop Cranmer, by gathering evidence that he was fostering heresy in Kent (which he was). But Henry refused the bait, and Cranmer survived, probably because of the king's abiding gratitude for his ready support in his various matrimonial crises. Cranmer had always been unhesitatingly loyal. Even when they had disagreed over justification, Cranmer had in the end yielded dutifully to the king's superior wisdom. A counter-coup in 1544 sought to implicate Gardiner in treason, but he likewise survived – although his nephew and secretary, Germain Gardiner, went to the block. Henry himself sought to stand above this endemic factional strife by adopting a pose of Olympian loftiness. He attached more and more importance to the rhetoric of the 'middle way', and in his public pronouncements, most notably in an address to Parliament in December 1545, he presented himself as the honest broker, as the wise Solomon protecting his Church from the squabbles of its own bishops and preachers, of whom, he said, invoking a recent scholarly proverb, 'some be too stiff in their old Mumpsimus, others be too busy and curious in their new Sumpsimus'.

The evangelicals regained some ground in the mid-1540s thanks to Henry's last marriage, to Catherine Parr. This could hardly have been predicted. Catherine had come to Court in the entourage of Princess Mary, and the early indications of her religious sympathies reveal her to have been essentially Catholic, although fashionably so. In her first years as queen she published a couple of books of prayers that came straight out of one of the main traditions of late medieval piety, the *devotio moderna* (or 'modern devotion'). However, she encountered other ideas at Henry's Court, and before long her original conservatism had given way to evangelical sympathies. She became the patroness of a project to translate the New Testament paraphrases of Erasmus into English. Erasmus's *Paraphrases* themselves were just about within the traditional bounds of Catholic orthodoxy, though he used them to promote criticisms of ecclesiastical abuses and popular superstition that many orthodox Catholics judged heretical. But the mind behind the translation project, Nicholas Udall, was a far more uncompromising figure. He dedicated the first instalment of the work to Catherine in September 1545, with an essay that not only endorsed every aspect of Henry's Reformation thus far but also portrayed that Reformation as a work in progress. And progress was clearly to be made, in his view, towards Protestantism. His preface urged the doctrine of justification by faith alone, in flat contradiction of the 'King's Book'. It is hardly surprising that he did not dare publish it while Henry lived. But it is revealing that he felt he could address such an openly evangelical text to Henry's queen without putting himself at risk.

Despite Henry's resolute refusal to advance down the path of Protestantism, and the continuing, if intermittent, persecution of Protestants, it has frequently been maintained that in fact he envisaged a more drastic Reformation, but through some insightful sensitivity to the ripeness of the times, realised that this would have to be a task for his son's rather than for his own reign. This is of course pure myth. Once the Protestant Reformation had been introduced after his death, there were many Protestant voices seeking to legitimise the abolition of the religion of the people – Catholicism – by the invocation of the still potent charisma of the late King Henry's memory. What is more puzzling is why modern historians have been so ready to echo them. The explanation probably lies in a combination of the modern myth of progress, in so many ways a secular reconfiguration of the Protestant myth of providence, with Henry's abiding grip on the national imagination. Could the great events that followed his death really have happened without his will or at least his foreknowledge? Surely not!

Yet indeed they did. For there is nothing to the idea beyond the mythopoeic appeal to intentionality, the notion that because it happened so soon after his death he 'must have' intended it. Certainly there is no evidence. All the relevant evidence points in a very different direction. Henry established his idiosyncratic religious synthesis in 1543, in the King's Book, which was buttressed with the authority of statute law. That same statute gave Henry the power to vary the synthesis at will. He never did so. Nor can we take very seriously the notion that he aspired to further religious change but felt that it would have to be accomplished by his son. No less an authority than Thomas Cranmer remarked after Henry's death that if Henry had decided to abolish the Mass – and abolishing or prohibiting the Mass was the decisive moment of any Protestant Reformation – then there was no one that could have withstood him.

The nearest thing to evidence for the thesis that Henry was happy to envisage religious change beyond what he had established is that he entrusted the education of his beloved son to Protestants. In a manner of speaking this is true. But only in a manner of speaking. Edward's tutors, Richard Cox and John Cheke, were both to become known as convinced Protestants. But this was not and could not be known in the early 1540s, when they were chosen to educate the prince. Richard Cox had actually been one of the half dozen men who drew up the final version of the King's Book in 1543. Although Cox may have been known to be on the evangelical wing of the church, Henry would hardly have suspected him of teaching his son anything contrary to the declaration of faith he had himself helped to draft. Cheke was certainly known to favour reform. He dedicated to the king a translation of a treatise by Plutarch, *On Superstition*, and his dedication showed his heartfelt approval for the king's campaigns against images and monasteries. But there was nothing in this to suggest that he would move even an inch beyond the king's position. And another translation that Cheke dedicated to the king, of selected extracts from the writings of Maximus the Confessor (a Greek theologian of the eighth century), included a clear denial of the crucial thesis of 'justification by faith alone'. Henry certainly had no reason to suspect that these men might teach his son another way than his own in religion. And given the awe and fear with which his subjects looked upon the aging king, there is no reason for us to suspect that they did. It would, quite literally, have been more than their lives were worth.

In 1546 Henry's declining health signalled that his reign was drawing to a close. Factional struggle intensified. Summer saw the conservatives in the ascendant. Anne Askew, a gentlewoman with connections to Catherine Parr and the court, was convicted of the sacramentarian heresy which Henry abominated, and the Lord Chancellor, Thomas Wriothesley, personally set his hand to the rack in his desperation to wring from her the information that would compromise evangelical rivals at court. But Anne gave him nothing of value. She was burned, along with a number of other heretics, in the presence of the Lord Chancellor and the Duke of Norfolk. Meanwhile, the bishop of London, Edmund Bonner, was striking fear into the heart of London's small but growing minority of Protestants, and heretical books were being burned as late as the end of September.

13

THE LAST DAYS: 1546 - 1547

By autumn, the pendulum was swinging the other way. The Duke of Norfolk's son, Henry Howard (Earl of Surrey), was foolish enough to flaunt his Plantagenet ancestry by quartering the royal arms into his own heraldic bearings – an act easily portrayed as treason in the charged atmosphere of the dying king's court. The Howards' rivals pounced, and the duke and the earl were both charged with treason, the earl for the act itself, and his father for not informing against him. The case rested, interestingly enough, on the powers of visitation and enquiry into heraldic bearings with which Henry VIII had invested the College of Arms (the corporation of royal heralds) in the 1520s. The new authority of the heralds was just one sign of how the relationship between Crown and nobility was changing, for it showed that the very concept of nobility was now dependent upon the king's will and pleasure. One of the 'Kings of Arms', thus established by their sovereign as arbiters of heraldic propriety, had warned Surrey against his heraldic pretensions – which were intended not as a claim to the throne but, more realistically, as a claim on his family's behalf, as the premier family in England, to exercise the regency for the young king who would soon succeed his father.

Henry Howard defended himself with such vigour that the jury hesitated long over their verdict. (His earldom was a courtesy title, not a peerage as such, so he was indicted before commoners at the Guildhall rather than before peers at Westminster.) However, William Paget rushed to court to seek the advice of his sovereign. On his return, he was allowed to interview the jurors, who promptly returned a guilty verdict. Even from his deathbed the ailing king could still overawe his subjects. Howard was beheaded on 19 January 1547, Henry's final victim. Rather than proceed by such means with the even flimsier case against the Duke of Norfolk, he was condemned by act of attainder a few days after his son's death. Destined for the scaffold on 28 January, he was saved only by the king's own death in the early hours of that morning. None of those scrabbling for power felt that anything short of the express and living royal will could command the execution of a duke.

As the end came, it was therefore the evangelicals who surrounded the dying king. In his will Henry endeavoured to provide collective government for his young son, nominating sixteen men to form Edward's Privy Council. But with the disgraced Howards excluded, along with their episcopal ally, 'wily Winchester', the shrewd Bishop Stephen Gardiner, the prospects of balance and stability among this group were slim. Asked why he had omitted Gardiner, the king explained that while he, Henry, could manage the bishop, nobody else could. The bishop, Henry reckoned, would end up running rings around the rest of them and taking sole charge. Henry's anxieties about the future were accurate in everything except their focus. The exclusion of Gardiner delivered Edward VI into the hands of his predatory uncle, Edward Seymour. Even so, Henry himself had no premonition of what would occur. Edward Seymour himself ingenuously admitted after Henry's death that the late king 'had very expressly commanded both him and all others of his Council to keep not only the laws but all else in the state of the realm in such condition as he had left them, without changing anything'. This express command is the most decisive evidence against the thesis that Henry contemplated with equanimity the prospect of a Protestant Reformation after his death. On the contrary, he probably envisaged his religious settlement as precisely that – a settlement. He really did think that he could rule from beyond the grave: it is a common delusion among tyrants.

Henry VIII died shortly after midnight, in the early hours of the morning of Friday 28 January. Had he died six months earlier, England would have remained a Catholic country. His own will encapsulated the ambiguities of his idiosyncratic religious compromise. Endowing a chantry for his soul at St George's Chapel, Windsor, where his splendid Renaissance tomb, cannibalised from Wolsey's, was still unfinished, and never to be finished, requesting thousands of Masses and seeking the intercession of the saints – Henry's imperious frame of mind is wonderfully expressed in the unselfconscious comment, 'we do instantly require the Blessed Virgin Mary ... to pray for us' – it could be the will of any late medieval king. Yet alongside this entirely traditional provision for his soul we can see the hand of Cranmer (or perhaps of Catherine Parr) guiding the royal pen into expressing confidence in evangelical terms:

> that every Christian creature living here in this transitory and wretched world under God, dying in steadfast and perfect faith... is ordained by Christ's Passion to be saved and to attain eternal life, of which number we verily trust by his grace to be one...

It was the conservative bishops Gardiner, Tunstall and Bonner who presided over the exequies of the king. Gardiner celebrated the requiem Mass on Sunday 13 February, and two days later presided over the arrival of Henry's coffin at Windsor Castle. The banners of St George, the patron saint of England, and of 'Good King Henry' (Henry VI), Henry's 'name saint', accompanied his funeral cortege as it made its way to the chapel of St George, where Henry VI himself was buried. For all his polemics against idolatry, Henry still inhabited the spiritual world of the old religion. But the old religion was to disown him as he had disowned the pope. Later Catholic historians reported that his coffin burst under the pressure of the rapid decomposition of his corpse, which therefore lay exposed, to be licked by dogs. Some added that Mary Tudor had him exhumed and burned, in the same way that he had dealt with Thomas of Canterbury. These stories, though, are but myths of vengeance against one for whom they felt the very fires of hell barely adequate. To Gardiner also it fell to preach the sermon at the burial on 16 February. Sadly, no text survives: it would have been illuminating to hear the final judgement on his master of a loyal servant who was at times so close to him. Henry was buried beside Jane Seymour, beloved among all his wives because she had given him a son.

LIST OF ILLUSTRATIONS

1500 1550 & © Jonathan Reeve JR1173b2p57B 1500 1550.

17. The *Harry Grâce à Dieu*. © Jonathan Reeve JR1180b20p814 1500 1550.

18. Cardinal Wolsey. © Jonathan Reeve JR1169b2p7 1500 1550.

19. Illuminated initial from the Plea Rolls, 1514. © Jonathan Reeve JR1183b20p885 1500 1550.

20. Erasmus. © Jonathan Reeve JR1160b4p600 1500 1550.

21. The Field of Cloth of Gold. © Jonathan Reeve JR1151b66p1 1500 1550.

22. *Pastyme with good companye*. Henry VIII's most famous song. © Jonathan Reeve JR1176b2p149 1500 1550.

23. & 24. The Field of Cloth of Gold. Two bas reliefs from the 1520s. © Jonathan Reeve JR1177b2p167B 1500 1550 & © Jonathan Reeve JR1177b2p167T 1500 1550.

25. An English Lady, by Holbein. © Elizabeth Norton and the Amberley Archive.

26. & 27. John More and Anne Cresacre, by Holbein. Both © Elizabeth Norton and the Amberley Archive.

28. The Family of Thomas More, by Holbein. © Elizabeth Norton and the Amberley Archive.

29. Elizabeth Dauncey, by Holbein. © Elizabeth Norton and the Amberley Archive.

30. Golden Bull of Pope Clement VII. © Jonathan Reeve JR1184b20p888 1500 1550.

31. Holbein's design for a jeweled pendant for Princess Mary. © Elizabeth Norton and the Amberley Archive.

32. Anne Boleyn's clock. © Jonathan Reeve JR1162b4p648 1500 1550.

33. Catherine of Aragon. By kind permission of Ripon Cathedral Chapter.

34. Henry VIII. © Josephine Wilkinson and the Amberley Archive.

35. Mary Boleyn. Courtesy of Hever Castle Ltd.

36. Treaty of Amiens, 18 August 1527. © Jonathan Reeve JR1182b20p881 1500 1550.

37. Hampton Court. © Jonathan Reeve JR1091b20p884 1500 1550.

38. Letter from Anne Boleyn to Wolsey. © Jonathan Reeve JR963b20p899 1500 1600.

39. A letter from Wolsey to the king, October 1529. © Jonathan Reeve JR1093b20p902 1500 1550.

40. Archbishop Warham, by Holbein. © Elizabeth Norton and the Amberley Archive.

41. Whitehall Palace. © Jonathan Reeve JR779b46fp192

and Fellows of St John's College, Cambridge.

64. Title-page of the Great Bible, 1539. © Jonathan Reeve JRCD2b20p929 15001550.

65. Act of Six Articles. © Jonathan Reeve JR1159b7p169 15001550.

66. Henry VIII as David. © Jonathan Reeve JR1164b4p663 15001550.

67. Anne of Cleves, by Barthel Bruyn. © Elizabeth Norton and the Amberley Archive.

68. Anne of Cleves House. © Elizabeth Norton and the Amberley Archive.

69. Nonsuch. © Jonathan Reeve JR1018b5fp204 15001550.

70. Mary Queen of Scots. © Jonathan Reeve JR1178b2fp440 15001550.

71. Hever Castle. © Elizabeth Norton and the Amberley Archive.

72. Oatlands (Surrey), one of Henry's many palaces. © Jonathan Reeve JR1149pc 15001550.

73. The Family of Henry VIII, ca. 1545. © Jonathan Reeve JR997b66fp40 15001550.

74. The Act of Succession, 1544. © Jonathan Reeve JR1185b20p920 15001550.

75. Design for a timepiece, by Holbein. © Elizabeth Norton and the Amberley Archive.

76. & 77. Henry VIII's will (30 December 1546) and Mary I. © Jonathan Reeve JRCD2b20p961 15501600 & by kind permission of Ripon Cathedral Chapter.

78. Henry VIII's signature. © Jonathan Reeve JR1150pc 15001550.

79. The 'Lady Elizabeth' of Henry VIII's later years. © Jonathan Reeve JR998b66fp56 15001600.

80. St George's Chapel, Windsor. © Jonathan Reeve JR1190b67plx 16001650.

81. Thomas Howard. © Jonathan Reeve JR1175b2p110 15001550.

INDEX

Tudor History from Amberley Publishing

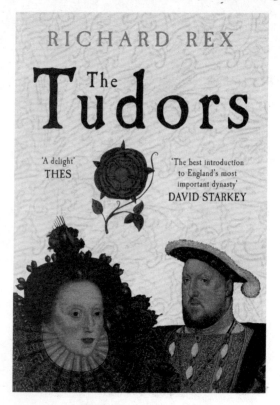